LEGAL STREET SMARTS

BY SCOT COURTNEY

BERKELEY PLACE BOOKS

Legal Street Smarts
By Scot Courtney
Cover illustrator: Mark Hoffer
Editor & book designer: Tom Johanningmeier
Book cover design: Kari Crane

Bulk sales of books from Wicked Smart Books/Great Texas Line Press are available at special discounts for fund raising, promotions and premiums.

Berkeley Place Books
An imprint of Great Texas Line Press
Post Office Box 11105
Fort Worth, Texas 76110
817-922-8929 / FAX 817-926-0420

This book is dedicated to:
My wife G
for her love, support and belief in me,
My mother
for lovingly instilling confidence in me,
And my mentor, Robert Scardino
for teaching me how to be an aggressive but ethical trial attorney

CONTENTS

INTRODUCTION

IF YOU ARE READING THIS, you are most likely in college, probably somewhere in Texas. Therefore this book was written taking certain assumptions to task. Unfortunately, our secondary educational system — the high schools — fail to educate students in some very basic areas that may impact you now and for the rest of your life. Really basic concerns are covered in this book to give you a rudimentary understanding of the law, how it works or doesn't work, and how it can and will impact your life. As you can see, the table of contents gives you the framework of areas I will discuss, and provides quick reference for those of you who have fallen into the time-honored, but deplorable habit of failing to read the entire book. That's OK, I've been there and that's exactly why I have written this book the way I have. Many of the areas covered I learned in college the hard way, some I learned afterward in law school or during my years of criminal law practice. Even others I only recently discovered when researching and writing this book. Almost every time, whether long ago or just yesterday, my usual reaction was, "Really? I didn't realize that." Or, "Oh shit!"

Knowledge is power. The more you know, the better prepared you are to deal with whatever situation you may find yourself. I hope this book answers those questions and can help you get through your college years without those "life experiences" so many of us had to endure. If not avoided altogether, you will be better equipped to deal with those situations to minimize any adverse effects.

Another concern in college is money. I was always looking for ways to get by on a budget, if you could call it that. So I have written the book with with the hope that the information may ultimately save you some bucks along the way. If money is not a problem, please excuse those passages; some of us need the help.

Likewise, this book deals with some areas that don't seem fair or right. I'm not telling you what is right or wrong, just what the law says. If you don't like it, please take the opportunity to write your representatives in Austin and Washington, D.C. Moral judgments, religious concerns or feelings of guilt and self-doubt will not enter into the posture in this book. I am an attorney and leave such areas to those who have an expertise in their areas, such as priests, psychiatrists, rabbis, psychologists, pastors, ministers or whomever you personally rely on for such areas of concern.

This book is not intended to be legal advice, but merely an overview of certain laws, legal terms and areas that may or may not address your exact and particular questions.

Usually there are variations and exceptions to these areas, and the laws are continually revised, repealed, amended and altered. Therefore the contents are based upon the status at the time of publication. It is strongly suggested that if you are unsure about what you should do in a particular situation, contact an attorney for legal advice or contact the legal services office at your university. Most universities have legal counsel on staff or can refer you to a lawyer who will not charge you for simple advice or counsel. Most lawyers will welcome the opportunity to at least discuss your problem or make suggestions without charging you one penny.

Meet Joe Butthead. Throughout the book, I'll refer to a fellow by the name of "Joe Butthead," Joe for short. You'll get to know our pal Joe real well over the coming pages, if you don't know him by some other name already. He's not based on one actual person, but rather an amalgam of many guys I knew in college, good and bad. I use him instead of the names of those who actually committed the crimes, behavior and activities detailed or referenced throughout this book. He is used to illustrate how the facts of a situation may be applied to the law and the various possible interpretations of the law. If Joe were a real person, he'd definitely be a permanent resident of the Texas prison system by now. Generally speaking, don't be like Joe. Learn from his bad manners and poor decision-making to avoid the mistakes he makes throughout this book.

CHAPTER 1
KICKED OFF CAMPUS

CAMPUS POLICE. The days of the rent-a-cop are over. Many college campuses have licensed police forces, many of them that investigate major crimes. So don't challenge a "campus cop," thinking he might not be a real cop. Like all peace officers, campus police have jurisdiction within the state and it extends far beyond campus. They're real cops, with real authority to use force.

Most campus law enforcement departments refer criminal charges to the criminal justice system, where prosecutors review them. Some campuses might handle low-level offenses through internal boards, tribunals or student courts. But any criminal allegation or arrest, especially on campus, can complicate a student's relationship with the university.

Code of conduct violations. Every college or university has rules and codes that their students are expected to follow. Whatever they're called — Code of Conduct, Student Conduct Code, Texas A&M's Aggie Code of Honor — they are simply rules established by the administration that you agree to follow as a condition of your admission and continued enrollment.

Simply put: follow these rules or you're out.

Usually, you are given these at freshman orientation and, whether you knew it or not, you acknowledged that you had read them and agreed to follow them. That's all great, until the school informs you that you must appear before the dean or a committee about some violation of the code.

I wish I could give detailed advice here, but every institution has some form of internal discipline over and above the legal process. Some are informal, some are conducted by deans or advisers, while others involve internal "courts" and boards and committees.

If you run afoul of the rules, know what the code is and review the procedures and potential punishments.

Many schools have begun to enforce these rules of conduct beyond their campuses, especially when they involve conflicts between students. Obviously, if you're traveling while representing the school, these codes are likely to apply. But enforcement of school rules beyond the campus have not been tested in the courts. I am not aware of any unreasonable enforcement, but it's a good idea to be mindful of the possibility.

Generally speaking, you have far fewer rights on campus if you're accused of wrongdoing or violating of a particular "code of conduct." But you're not defenseless in your "right" to remain enrolled. The problem is that the Supreme Court has determined that an education is not a "right," but rather a privilege. Therefore, you can be stripped of that privilege with broad discretion. That being said, an administration cannot arbitrarily exercise its particular brand of authority as it seems fit.

Public schools, more than private institutions, must comply with the notions of general fairness that flirts with what we call "due process." This is because the government is much more involved in the funding and administration of a public school. Most public colleges' codes of conduct try to provide for such, but they fall woefully short of constitutional due process.

If you're faced with suspension or expulsion from a public institution, you should expect and demand:

- That your case be heard in accordance with the established, adopted and published rules and procedures used for such cases.
- That you receive proper and reasonable notice of the rules that are alleged to have been violated.
- That you are provided a description, report, statement or other similar form that describes the evidence supporting the alleged violation.

- A forum to present your side of the story to an impartial body, panel or committee.

The disciplinary process may start with an informal interview by an administrator, who can resolve the matter with some form of resolution and who might then make recommendations to a higher board or panel for further review.

Some campus' student justice panels or peer-review committees are comprised of diverse representatives of the campus population in an effort of inclusion.

Be sure to know your campus' procedures and take advantage of the limited "right" it may afford you.

Private universities have broad latitude in who they admit, the conditions of continued enrollment and the reasons for expulsion or suspension. Nonetheless, they too must have procedures in place to protect themselves from the appearance or allegations of discriminatory enforcement of their rules.

It is important to understand that since there is no right to "due process," your constitutional protections are severely affected. For example, Fourth Amendment protection against unreasonable search and seizure, freedom of speech, the right to legal representation and other recognized and staunchly held rights simply are diluted in this part of the system.

Drugs "illegally" seized from an "illegal" entry into a dorm room by campus police may very well be used to expel you from school, but the same evidence is forbidden for criminal prosecution.

Though the right to due process is not recognized as such in these "on-campus" administrative actions, they do serve and important purpose relating to due process. Once you have exhausted the administrative remedies, you can go to the formal judicial system. Now the right to due process cloaks you in the process.

If you find yourself accused, know your "rights" under the system and protect yourself. Consulting with an attorney, even if he is barred from the interview or hearing, can give you insight and suggestions in how to prepare and proceed. Be proactive: Don't simply think it will fade away. If the allegations involve drugs or alcohol, submit to private drug testing and provide clean tests to demonstrate that you do not consume illegal drugs. If it involves alcohol, do the same or consult with a counselor to recommend a course of actions that would demonstrate you are addressing whatever problems a professional has identified. Anger management issues or concerns can be addressed through some form of counseling, as well. Remember that the university simply wants its students and the campus atmosphere to function at the highest level it can foster. It wants to keep everyone safe and, most of all, to make sure administrators and the school are not perceived as "doing nothing."

Lastly, some of these rules and codes have built-in "self-reporting" requirements. Some require that the student notify the administration of "off-campus" arrests or violations. Failure to report can be the actual cause of the disciplinary action, even if the over-arching conditions or behavior is not. If a situation arises that you think may trigger this, consult with an attorney to discuss for more guidance.

Trespassing on campus. The fact that public colleges and universities are government buildings on public property does not mean that you cannot be asked to leave, even if you are a student, alumni, employee, or visitor. If you're not following the institution's rules and policies, you may be asked to leave. If you ignore repeated instructions to leave, you run the risk go being charged and issued a criminal trespass warning.

Criminal trespassing is covered at the end of Chapter 10, however the Texas Education Code specifically authorizes a state university or college to "refuse to allow persons having no legitimate business to enter on property under the board's control, and may eject any undesirable person from the property on his refusal to leave peaceably on request. Identification may be required of any person on the property."

The mix of public spaces with restricted areas (not to mention the public nature of the common areas, walkways and roadways) makes this a difficult area to navigate. Private institutions can control who comes onto the campus, who stays and who must leave. The same rules of trespassing apply to private campuses as they do to private property.

People cannot be kept from public streets, common areas and parks unless they are breaking the law, violating campus rules, have no legitimate business or are generally loitering.

Academic suspension. Academic suspension or expulsion is a different story.

Simply put, if you don't make the grade, you're out. The school has a huge degree of control over whether you stay or go. Stay on those grades and if you are having trouble, seek out all of the school's resources, such as tutoring, after-hour study reviews, and graduate-assistant reviews.

If you have a physical, medical, or psychological problem, especially a learning disability that directly affects your ability to attend or perform the work required, seek out the resources of the university and request that accommodations be made to address your specific issues. Do not be embarrassed or ashamed. Bring it to the attention of the administration, the dean or your professor sooner than later. This way, it can be acknowledged, documented and addressed before it becomes a bigger problem or simply looks like an excuse later.

CHAPTER 2
YOUR LEGAL RIGHTS

COPS AND THEIR AUTHORITY

I THINK EVERYONE can agree that one of the hardest, most stressful and dangerous jobs in the world is that of a police officer. They have to deal with people most of us would never want to meet in any situation, much less at times and in places that are just plain scary. They are an essential cog in our society's peaceful and safe operation.

But as it is with any profession, a few bad cops can make it bad for the whole bunch. There are some tips to follow that not only will reduce your chances for arrest, but also ensure that the officers doing their job properly are given the respect and dignity they deserve from you.

These tips are offered with the U.S. and Texas constitutions in mind:

Always be respectful of officers. A policy of "Yes Sir/No Sir" will serve you well. Don't offer small talk or excuses. Just answer the officer's questions and peacefully comply with his requests. Don't cop an attitude because you're inconvenienced or argue the law; he or she will not appreciate it and may decide that you need to be taught some manners, a lesson that requires a night in jail.

You have a much better chance of being sent on your way if you show that you're a polite, reasonable, safe and law-abiding individual. According to the Texas Department of Public Safety, when stopped by a law enforcement officer, DPS recommends that you:

- Keep your hands in plain sight.
- Cooperate fully with the police officer.
- If you have a gun with you, tell the officer as soon as possible.
- Don't make any quick movements, especially toward the weapon.
- At night, turn on your vehicle's dome light.

I tend to agree with most of this advice, but I will leave it to you to decide what is and is not good advice based on what is covered later.

Never physically resist or avoid an officer's grasp or interfere with an officer's actions, much less strike an officer. This is likely to result in a charge of resisting arrest or assault of a peace officer, with more serious charges coming if a weapon is used. Historically speaking, these volatile situations have resulted in the death of people at the hands of arresting officers.

Never run away. You run the risk of being charged with evading detention or arrest. If you're in a car, it's a felony with escalating degrees of punishment for various "police chase" situations, including a second-degree felony if someone is killed as a result of your flight. There's also a chance the officers might decide (or even be authorized) to use deadly force to apprehend you.

Avoiding an officer or erratic driving will usually result in an officer stopping you and asking questions, if for nothing else than your "suspicious" behavior. Immediately walking away or running when a cop pulls up is a sure-fire way to get run down and "detained" for questioning.

Don't step in to help out your buddy who has just been arrested, much less help him break the chains of bondage and run away. You expose yourself to the possibility of joining your friend in the back seat of the cop car, and could face several offenses, including permitting or facilitating escape or hindering apprehension or prosecution. The best thing you can do for your friend is to contact the jail and try to bail him out first thing in the morning.

Don't make a bad situation worse. It is not a defense to any of the above-detailed offenses that the arrest itself was a false arrest. Try to minimize your potential criminal exposure. Remember the old saying, "You can beat the rap, but you won't beat the ride."

You may ask, "What the hell does that mean?"

It means that even if you're not convicted, you will nonetheless suffer the humiliation, degradation and inconvenience that comes with spending a night in jail.

Cops and their authority. All peace officers are held to the same requirements regarding how they can intrude upon and pry into someone's life. State police officers may be further restricted by state constitutions, but generally the U.S. Constitution gives us the best and most reliable guidepost.

A popular misconception is that an officer who is outside his geographic jurisdiction loses his authority as a peace officer. In Texas, certified peace officers have the authority to act anywhere in the state and are considered to always be "on duty," whether they're actually "on duty" or not. That authority does not extend beyond the state line but a federal agent's jurisdiction extends throughout the country.

Race and some harsh realities. Just in case you hadn't heard: Life is not fair.

Racism, prejudices and inequality are harsh realities, and it must be taken into account when you're interacting with police officers.

We've seen the videos showing tragic interactions between police and citizens, many of them of color. A statistical analysis by the Washington Post suggests that more than 100 people were shot and killed by police after a traffic stop in 2015; one in three were black. Considering that black people are disproportionately more likely to be stopped, their risks of finding themselves in a potentially dangerous situation are exponentially greater than the population as a whole.

No matter the reasons behind the statistics, people of color are at greater risk of being stopped, searched, arrested, sent to prison and, apparently, shot. This is a reality that must be addressed on many fronts, but the most immediate concern is you and your knowledge of how to best react to certain situations so you can avoid these unjust byproducts of the current state of affairs.

Most, if not all, of the suggestions in this book are applicable to everyone, no matter your race. But if you are black, brown, Middle Eastern or in any way resemble a class of people that is stereotypically considered threatening, then pay close attention to the suggestions in this book to protect yourself. The sooner you can identify what particular bias or obstacles are against you, the sooner you can address how to avoid them or even tip the balance in your favor.

"AS SEEN ON TV"

So you have been stopped, arrested or charged with a crime. What are your rights and what can you do? First off, we will go through the typical Miranda Warning that everyone has heard a hundred times in the movies and on TV.

"You are under arrest for (insert charge); you have the right to remain silent; anything you say or do may be and most likely will be used against you at a trial for this or any other offense; you have the right to an attorney, if you cannot afford an attorney, one will be provided for you; you may give up these rights and speak to an officer."

There are hundreds of variations of this warning, but the gist is to let you know that you are under arrest and you do not have to say or do anything. You can refuse to answer questions at any time, even if you are stopped in your car or are walking down the street.

A popular misconception is the arrest will be tossed if the police fail to "read you your rights." It may affect what evidence is admissible in court, namely statements made by you in response to questioning, but all in all that's about it. That's not to say that a good trial attorney won't use such a breach to your advantage at trial, but it probably won't get your case thrown out of court.

IN THE REAL WORLD

Is identification required? Known as "stop and identify" statutes, some state laws require citizens to disclose their name when requested by a law enforcement officer.

Texas has no such statute. If you have been detained, but not arrested, you don't have to give police squat, but refusing to identify yourself might cause them to arrest you anyway so they can determine who you really are.

You are not legally required to carry a driver's license or other ID if you're not driving, but it is a crime to give false information about your identity, whether you've been arrested or just detained. If you've been arrested, you have to give your name, address, and date of birth to a police officer who requests it. They'll probably ask you for lots more than this, but these three items are all you're legally required to give. If you answer questions, remember: whatever you say probably will be used as evidence later.

Your right to remain silent. The Fifth Amendment to the U.S. Constitution guarantees that a no person "shall be compelled in any criminal case to be a witness against himself."

Generally speaking, any statement made by someone in custody in response to questions by the police cannot be used against that person unless he has been informed of his rights and he has waived those rights. But any statement made — with or without the warning — that was not in response to a question is not protected.

So the best policy is that once you are under arrest, you should not say anything other than to identify yourself and request to speak with an attorney. This also applies to other people, such as others who are under arrest, whom you may feel compelled to "tell your story" to while in jail or the back seat of the patrol car.

If the police officers or investigators become aggressive or threaten you, remain resolute in your determination not to answer their questions. They're not there "to help you" nor do they have any authority to "make you a deal" or "go easy on you." Only the prosecutor has the authority to do so, so don't fall for their trap.

The U.S. Supreme Court has held that it is OK for the police to lie to you and trick you into talking or confessing. They still can't beat you, at least for now, nor can they withhold food, water or other essentials for life. But they can make it extremely uncomfortable and unpleasant, so your best bet and probably quickest way out of the interrogation situation is to continue to refuse to answer any question and ask for an attorney in a polite and respectful manner, repeatedly if necessary. (See the *I Wanna Talk To My Attorney* section below.)

The Fifth Amendment also applies to trials. The choice to testify is up to the accused and they cannot be called by the state to testify against themselves. A person who has been subpoenaed to testify as a witness must testify, unless he has a privilege not to. There are privileges for spouses, doctors, reporters and attorney-client communications. Typically, a person who is asked questions that may incriminate himself may assert his Fifth Amendment right not to answer.

Why not just explain and they'll let me go? They might, but don't bank on it. For those of you who have asked this question, God love you for your trusting soul, but I am here to tell you: Statements made just after arrest, during police questioning and sometimes at trial from the witness chair, can be some of the most damning evidence.

There are some things that you need to understand:

- The people who have stopped you and are questioning you (the cops) are already convinced that you have done something illegal.
- They will probably not believe what you have to say unless it helps to confirm their belief.
- They are there to gather evidence against you.
- You will probably see them at your trial and they will not be there to testify for you.
- At trial, even a marginal prosecutor can make a defendant look bad through good cross-examination.
- The courtroom is like a public speech in front of a big audience; a witness can make a bad impression on the jury for any number of reasons, such as: cockiness, nervousness, anxiety, shyness, a speech disorder, a lack of education, or any number of factors that may justify a defendant's reason not to testify other than his or her guilt.

I got a subpoena. A right afforded to the prosecution, parties to civil lawsuits and the accused citizen is the right to compulsory process, which is the power to make witnesses appear and testify. A subpoena is the legal instrument that makes this happen. It is a common misconception that a subpoena has no "legal" effect unless it is actually placed in one's hands. This is not the case. There are various ways that a person can be forced to appear and testify: Certified mail, faxes, phone calls and other methods have been ruled adequate, so if you have received or been informed of a subpoena requiring your attendance against your wishes, consult an attorney to discuss your options, as well as the testimony that is being sought.

Ignoring a subpoena is not the smart thing to do. If a witness does not appear as ordered by the subpoena, an arrest warrant may be issued.

"I WANNA TALK TO MY LAWYER"

Right to a lawyer. You certainly have the right to legal counsel at any time that you choose. This does not mean that after the police officer has arrested you he will immediately take you by your dad's attorney's office or hand you his cell phone. Even if you continue to ask for an attorney, you may not actually get to talk with one for several hours, if not longer.

The bad news. Usually you are not free to just pick up the phone, because you are being arrested AND it's 2 a.m. AND you know your dad's golfing buddy Mr. Cheatham, the lawyer, is fast asleep AND the cops know this AND they don't really care AND they would rather have you on videotape extremely pissed off and irrational rather than poised and courteous. It's a bit of a Catch-22: You may request an attorney, but the police don't have to let you have one or talk to one for quite some time.

The good news. Your request to speak with an attorney may affect what they do or don't do with you and may affect the admissibility of any statements you make after that point. Similar to the *Right To Remain Silent* section discussed above, the basic rule is that once you inform the arresting police officer, the investigating agent or a similar "state" official that you wish to speak with an attorney, they should not continue with any form of questioning that might bring responses that could incriminate you. Be courteous but resolute in your decision not to answer their questions and request to speak with an attorney, repeatedly if necessary, if you decide to exercise these rights.

When is it legally required that you're given an attorney? If you have been arrested, have not made bail and can't afford an attorney, you have the right to have one provided to you. Some courts have begun to take the position that if a person has made bail, he can afford to hire an attorney. But this is not the law and everyone has the right to have an attorney provided if they are indigent and cannot afford one.

"I need a lawyer, but i don't know any." The best way to find an attorney is by referral. Hopefully you know an attorney or know someone who knows one. Surfing the 'net has become the "go-to" option and most reputable attorneys have a presence online. That said, ask around. Your friends, professors, co-workers and family should give you a start. Most universities have legal counsel on campus that can answer questions and, in some instances, even represent you.

"How do I find a good one?" Get a few names, make appointments and go talk to several attorneys before writing a check. Find one you are comfortable with and can talk to. If you get a letter from an attorney in the mail after an arrest, I suggest you throw it away. I have never heard a positive story from someone who hired one of these "cut rate" lawyers. Any reputable attorney should at least be willing to give you a few minutes of their time for free. If not, they are probably too busy to devote the time to your case to your satisfaction, so move on. Ask plenty of questions. If the lawyer can't answer your questions, or at least give you a good reason why he can't, move on.

Remember, if it sounds too good to be true, it probably is. Any lawyer who guarantees the outcome cannot be trusted. He is either lying to you or involved in something you don't want to be involved in. That also goes for price. You get what you pay for. Be very circumspect of an attorney who charges a fee substantially lower than those you have talked with. Sometimes, your pocketbook makes these decisions, but always consider all aspects of the case, your budget, your priorities and your expectations, not only in the immediate future, but also in the long-term. This is another good reason to talk with several attorneys, so you can get an idea of what the market price is and make your choices accordingly.

SEARCH AND SEIZURE

Any restriction in a citizen's freedom of movement or detention by the government is an "arrest" or rather a "seizure" of one's person. A "search" is any intrusion into a citizens' "zone of privacy." That is any area in which a reasonable person may expect privacy from the public. Any arrest or search of a citizen is considered unreasonable unless the officers conducting the arrest and search have probable cause to do so.

Probable cause and reasonable suspicion. The reasonable suspicion requirement is just one of many "checks" that help to ensure that citizens are not subjected to unreasonable searches and seizures as protected by the Fourth Amendment and the Texas Constitution. Before an officer can stop and detain a person, he must have reasonable suspicion (specific facts to reasonably suspect that the person stopped is associated with criminal activity).

Your car. In order to search someone's vehicle, an officer must have probable cause.

We see Joe Butthead cruising down the road in his 1988 Dodge Diplomat, with the NORML sticker on the bumper, tinted windows, and red tape covering one of the cracked taillights.

Joe is headed to pick up his date for dinner and a movie. Joe has his favorite Snoop Dog song blaring and the windows rolled down. As Joe rolls through the stop sign that no one ever stops at, a police cruiser's lights flash in Joe's rearview. He immediately pulls over to a safe place, signaling (of course) and comes to a stop. The officer has reasonable suspicion to stop Joe (the stop sign violation), but the reality is that the NORML sticker, the loud music and the tinted windows probably didn't help Joe slide by without a stop.

Joe is smart and follows all the advice discussed in Chapter 1 but the officer still asks him to step out of the car. Joe complies and the officer now asks him a series of questions.

"You been drinkin'?"

"What's your hurry?"

"Where you going?"

"You got anything in your car that I need to know about? Drugs or guns?"

"You mind if I look in your car?"

At this point, bells and whistles should be going off in Joe's head. Although Joe doesn't personally smoke the noxious weed himself, Joe's roommate regularly borrows the "sweet ride" for dates and has been known to "smoke a joint" every now and then.

Now Joe considers his options:

- If Joe gives consent to the officer to search his car, whatever is found can be used against him.
- If Joe refuses, the only way the officer can legally search is if he has probable cause or a reasonable suspicion to do so.

But if the officer smells or claims later to have smelled "a distinct odor that through his training and experience smells like burnt or burning marijuana" then he probably has probable cause or knows how to create probable cause to search Joe's car. Otherwise he would have to get a warrant to search or have some justification to arrest Joe. Lo and behold, he finds a "roach" or "extinguished marijuana cigarette" under the seat, where your moron, stoned roommate missed throwing it out the window the last time he borrowed your car.

BANG, Joe is under arrest for Class B misdemeanor possession of marijuana.

If you loan your car to your stoner friends, you better keep it clean or you may pay for their fun with a night in the pokey. The real moral of the story is if you choose to express yourself through the appearance of your car, expect to get pulled over more often than you would if you were driving your mom's minivan. Scrape the NORML sticker off, turn down the Kid Rock and make sure your inspection and registration stickers are valid, as well as all lights, license plate and other "chicken-shit" reasons that may give an officer reason to stop you. Maybe even make a donation to the local police officer association. They usually give you one of those "I support the Badge" type of window decals; stick it on, you need all the help you can get.

Yourself. Before a police officer can "frisk" you, he has to have some form of reasonable suspicion to stop you. The officer is authorized to "pat you down" to make sure you're not armed. He may not reach inside your pockets unless he feels something that he knows by the "pat-down" to be a weapon or contraband (drugs). If you are under valid arrest, he can search anywhere.

Joe is walking down the street, dressed in his favorite flip-flops and jeans, his mohawk blowing in the wind and the bitchin' tattoo on his shoulder is blazin' in the afternoon sun when a patrol car stops next to Joe and an officer gets out and approaches him. Joe remembers from Chapter 1, Don't run off or try to obviously avoid him. This will get the officer's attention every time.

The officer walks over to Joe and asks a couple of harmless questions.

"How's it going?"

"What's up?"

Joe relaxes, because he knows he is a reasonable and responsible guy out for a walk, just heading home after classes. Joe just talks to the officer, remembering to be polite. Joe doesn't give him a reason to be suspicious. He now asks for some ID. Joe reaches in his pocket because he knows he should always have some form of picture ID, just in case.

"Oh shit."

Joe has forgotten his ID.

"What? No ID? Hands on the car."

And the officer begins to pat Joe down.

Joe is smart enough not carry a weapon or drugs so the officer doesn't feel anything suspicious. Joe gives him his driver's license number and date of birth.

The officer goes to his car and runs Joe's info. He comes back over, and:

Joe goes home. He tells Joe that he is sorry for the inconvenience and to have a nice day.

Joe goes to jail. BANG, Joe forgot about that speeding ticket last summer and it's gone to warrant. The officer searches Joe and finds that "roach" in his cigarette pack and the "dime bag" of weed in Joe's backpack. BANG, BANG, Joe is charged with a new misdemeanor and there really isn't much Joe's attorney will have to contest the search, because of the warrant and valid arrest.

Joe's story gets interesting. But that wasn't Joe's ticket. His roommate stole Joe's ID to go clubbing last year and got the ticket. Unless Joe can convince him to admit to the charge of false ID to peace officer or there is a picture of his roommate being arrested, Joe is probably gonna eat it.

Joe's story takes another turn. Joe was on top of his game and took care of his business and paid that ticket. Joe's attorney does his homework and verifies that the warrant in the computer was not lifted because of the county's carelessness. Joe's attorney is bright enough to fashion a constitutional argument that the search was not incident to a valid arrest and the evidence of weed in Joe's backpack should be suppressed. Joe's attorney kicks some serious legal ass and Joe walks.

Your house and home. Generally speaking, an officer cannot enter your home without without a search warrant or arrest warrant. But he may enter your home if he sees something "in plain view" that constitutes a crime. This situation usually comes up when an officer is dispatched to a loud music complaint. The officer knocks on the door, and a cloud of smoke bellows out when Joe Butthead opens it. Through the open door, the officer sees Joe's buddies sitting around the living room with a bong on the coffee table. In this situation, the officer may enter, seize the bong and marijuana, and generally may arrest whomever he determines possessed the contraband, maybe even everyone.

"I think I'll just invite a few people over." Great idea. Joe has a party. It is huge: people in and out, spilling into the yard, cars parked up and down both sides of the street. The cops show up and barge into the house, whereupon they see alcohol being consumed and several underage girls drinking, not to mention the half-smoked joint on the kitchen table.

The officer's entry into the house generally would be considered unreasonable. However, the presence of so many people freely entering and exiting the house and the underage drinking will probably give rise to the prosecution's argument that Joe's house was "open to the public" and therefore the officers merely entered into a public space.

Now let's say that Joe's next party is not quite so big and is contained entirely inside the house. The cops show up and knock on the door. Joe answers, and the cops tell him the music is too loud and asks if they can enter.

"No, you can't enter, but I will turn down the music," Joe tells them.

The cops come inside anyway. They are not authorized in this situation and any arrest or evidence they seize may be subject to exclusion or legal attack and suppression.

Take the same situation, but when Joe tells the cops no, they tell him they will be getting a warrant and will be back in 30 minutes.

That may or may not be true.

The cops will probably not be able to get a warrant based upon the information they have. They must have probable cause to support the warrant, which would be questionable. Joe is certainly under no obligation to allow the officers in. If he consents to let them in and they find something that exposes Joe to criminal prosecution, Joe cannot later complain that the officers didn't have a warrant because they entered with his permission.

Only a person who has a "possessory interest" in a house or car can give consent to enter to search. That means that a person who owns, rents or is a guest actually staying in a house, apartment or even a hotel room all have a possessory interest in the property and can consent to a search or entry.

Consent to search? Just say "no"! You have a constitutional right to just say "no" to any officer who asks for your permission to search you, your car or your residence.

Remember, once an officer has your permission to enter, whatever he sees in "plain view" is fair game. Sometimes a refusal will bring threats to get a warrant or drug dog, but if the officer really had probable cause to search, he would not be asking for your consent. If a search is reasonable under the law, an officer does not require your permission to search, but once your permission is given, the search is lawful, even without probable cause. All evidence obtained may be admissible against you. When in doubt, just say "no."

Why should you just say "no" to a request to search when you have nothing to hide? A reasonable search is based on an officer's knowledge that probable cause existed before the search and seizure. Your permission justifies the search, even an unreasonable search, but your refusal places the burden on the officer to demonstrate in court that the officer knew enough to justify a reasonable search before the search was conducted. Always remember that not all police officers are trustworthy and some have been known to stretch the truth on occasion to make arrests and convictions.

"Reasonable" searches and seizures are:

- Authorized by lawfully issued search warrants.
- Incidental to lawful arrests.
- Based on probable cause.
- Conducted with voluntary, express and specific consent.

Cops are not required to inform you that you have a constitutional right to refuse to allow a search and a refusal cannot be used to imply probable cause of criminal activity. Most times, officers are not really looking for anything in particular and they rely on peoples' ignorance to get the consent to look around. A good rule of thumb when asked for consent to search is to tell the officer: "Officer, I don't have anything to hide, but I don't want you pawing through my stuff."

What if they come in anyway? If an officer enters your home or car without your consent, there are couple of practical things you should do:

- Remain calm and courteous, but challenge the officer's right and authority to enter your property by asking why he is entering without your consent. Even ask the officer to leave, but do it politely.
- If an officer requests permission to search you, your vehicle or your home, you should say, "No, sir; please get a warrant."
- Document every aspect that you believe constitutes illegal conduct or discourteous, unprofessional or abusive conduct by writing a letter or filing a formal complaint. Include the identity of each person who witnessed the incident, as well as their own handwritten account, if possible.
- Consult a reputable attorney as soon as possible to discuss the officer's actions.

FREE SPEECH

You wander into your coffee house one morning and you first see her. Long, unmade, dark hair. Elvis Costello glasses. She's sipping coffee, while apathetically reading the campus rag. Disgusted with the world, she tosses her paper on the table and trudges out. Over the next few weeks you hang at the coffee house until you find an opportunity to talk to her and BANG, you're in love.

Lola is her name. Beautiful, dark, loud and pissed off at the world, this chick has convinced you that meat-eaters and fur- and leather-wearers are evil and must be stopped. Lola has convinced you through advanced brainwashing techniques, such as prolonged periods of wild sex, that you should help her and her "vegan" freak friends when they decide to mount a protest in the Quad.

You arrive at the appointed time and begin to voice your (her) opinions regarding the evils of meat, fur, and even leather goods. Lola hands you a bucket of red paint and instructs you to voice those same opinions while hurling red paint on each person who walks by wearing leather or fur. Just to emphasize free-speech rights, someone whips out a U.S. flag and begins to burn it. It's quite a protest you've got going on when the campus police arrive and the kiss of steel wraps around your wrists.

BANG, you're under arrest.

But why? Protest and free speech is the only way to bring about social change and raise the public consciousness. All true, but as you will see, absolute protection is not guaranteed. You may be facing charges such as assault, criminal mischief and inciting riot in addition to the violations of campus policies.

I'm not telling you that public protest and speech is not a good thing. Free speech, the expression of ideas and civic protest are a few of my favorite things and is a valid and legal way to make your opinions known. But there are limitations on the way that you go about it. If your message is that important, find a way to lawfully express it. If not, I at least admire your convictions, if not the message. Some things are important enough to go to jail over, if they are expressed peacefully and for the right reasons.

First Amendment. *Congress shall make no law respecting an establishment of religion, or prohibiting the free exercise thereof; or abridging the freedom of speech, or of the press; or the right of the people peaceably to assemble, and to petition the Government for a redress of grievances.*

— The First Amendment to the U.S. Constitution

Without the First Amendment, religious minorities would be persecuted, protesters would be forcibly silenced, the press could not criticize the government, and the citizens could not demand or effect social change.

School-sponsored prayer, the Pledge of Allegiance, and the removal of religious figures from public buildings are a few issues we see in the media that impacts the rights of free speech and religion. Religious liberty and tolerance are constantly pitted against conflicting religious beliefs, the law, or a citizen's right to be free from forced exposure to another citizen's religious practice or beliefs. Historically, other issues have come and gone, but the hallmark to resolving these issues, ironically, is the freedom itself. The right to freely express and debate one's views usually contributes to the ultimate resolution, whatever the resolution may be. These sorts of difficulties are the price of freedom of speech and religion in a tolerant, open society. That said, ask yourself, Are we as a nation as tolerant as we like to think we are?

The Supreme Court has never said that all speech is protected, but political speech apparently enjoys the most protection, while commercial and obscene speeches have a lessened degree of freedom. A citizen does not have a right to say anything at any time in any place. In some instances, what is or is not "speech" is an important element in determining the degree of freedom associated with the speech, but also it is the distinction between speech and conduct that may impact Supreme Court decisions interpreting these issues. Speech that is part of an otherwise illegal act enjoys no protection and "hate speech" continues to draws the eye of the Supreme Court each October.

College campuses have been especially active in restricting free speech the past 30 years. Many limit public speech and expression, including the use social media. Check your school's policies before taking to the streets. If you feel those restrictions infringe on your rights, make your voice heard and try to change them. If not, go get your message out.

Try to find ways to make your point without trampling on the rights of others, especially on campus. Consider reading some of the writings and teachings of Mahatma Ghandi regarding passive resistance or Martin Luther Kings' writings on civil disobedience and non-violent protest. They were quite effective in getting their points across and bringing about great social and political change in relatively short periods of time. Be committed to your beliefs, but remember to listen to others and, most important, respect their right to hold, debate, disagree and express those opinions you disagree with.

Some criminal limitations on free speech:

- Obstructing highway or other passageway is a charge that is usually used to disperse protests and demonstrations. It's a Class B misdemeanor and occurs when someone obstructs a street or passageway
- Disrupting meeting or procession. Anyone who prevents or disrupts a lawful meeting, procession commits a Class B misdemeanor.
- Riot is the gathering of seven or more people that creates an immediate danger of damage to property or injury to people, or that substantially obstructs law enforcement or other governmental functions or services. It is also using force or the threat of force to deprive someone of a legal right or disturbing any person in the enjoyment of a legal right.
- False alarm or report. Making a false report (bomb, fire, etc.) is a Class A misdemeanor; it's a state jail felony if it involves a school, utility or public communications.

CHAPTER 3
CRIME AND PUNISHMENT

CLASSIFICATION OF CRIMES AND OFFENSES

MISDEMEANORS PUNISHMENT RANGE:

Class A: Up to one year in county jail and $4,000 fine.

- Class B: Up to six months in county jail and $4,000 fine.
- Class C: No jail. Up to $500 fine.

Felonies punishment range:

- Capitol felony: Life in prison or death penalty.
- First degree: Life in prison or five to 99 years in prison and up to $10,000 fine.
- Second degree: Two to 20 years in prison and up to $10,000 fine.
- Third degree: Two to 10 years in prison and up to $5,000 fine.
- State jail felony: 180 days to two years in state jail and up to $10,000 fine.

Note: The above punishment ranges do not reflect the possibility for probation or deferred adjudication, nor do they reflect enhanced punishments for offenders who have prior convictions.

Probation. Now referred to as community supervision, it is generally available for those who have limited or no criminal history with numerous variations, depending on the offense and the individual. Community supervision is available for all misdemeanor offenses and most felonies with sentences of ten years or less. Someone placed on community supervision agrees to follow the conditions set by the judge. Failure to do so can result in revocation or adjudication, which allows the judge to sentence the probationer to up to the maximum punishment in jail.

It is important to remember that anyone who pleads guilty and receives community supervision has waived or given up the vast majority of his rights and protections under the law.

Deferred adjudication. There is one basic difference between probation and deferred adjudication. Deferred adjudication results in the offense being dismissed once the individual completes the supervision. It is not erased from the records, but the records do reflect that it was dismissed. Therefore, if it was a felony, the person has not been convicted of a felony and retains certain civil rights upon the completion of his term of supervision.

THE BAGGAGE OF CONVICTION

Those convicted of a felony lose the right to vote and own and use a firearm. A drug conviction (even a small one for marijuana possession) can prevent you from receiving grants, scholarships and financial aid, as well as other government benefit. It may affect your ability to acquire state licenses, such as law, aviation, real estate and certified public accountant.

A recent development concerns sex offender registration with the state of Texas and local police agencies. Numerous sex-related convictions may require registration as a sex offender for life.

Speeding and other minor infractions. A speeding ticket and almost all traffic violations are Class C misdemeanors, which means that you cannot be put in jail if convicted. But if you refuse to sign the ticket, the police officer has no choice but to arrest you to make sure you appear before a judge.

Other Class C misdemeanors include trespassing, disorderly conduct, certain alcohol violations, noise and nuisance violations and assault by offensive speech and/or contact. The most important thing is to take care of it. If you don't or if you fail to appear, a warrant will be issued and the next time you are stopped you will most likely be arrested and have to make a bond. That is usually the amount equal to the maximum fine of the ticket and a "warrant fee." And you'll likely be stopped and arrested at the most inconvenient time possible, like right before an exam or, God forbid, when you really don't want the cop to search your car, which they always do when someone is arrested.

You wouldn't believe how many more serious offenses are filed after a search when someone is arrested for warrants. Oh yeah, and you can't contest the search, because the warrant basically gives the cops the right to search for just about anything.

Class C misdemeanors usually don't carry too much baggage, unless they are thefts or offenses involving alcohol. These types of offenses usually have habitual violator enhancements that allow the prosecution to elevate to level of offense for repeated violations. Repeated speeding or moving offenses will be covered later in the *Speeding Tickets And Other Moving Violations* section.

Crimes of moral turpitude. A crime of moral turpitude is generally a crime of dishonesty, baseness or vileness.

A person convicted of a crime of moral turpitude should expect barriers to licensing and employment in professions such as finance, law, accounting, securities and any job requiring that the person be bondable and act as a fiduciary. Examples of these types of offenses are:

- Any offense against a person with intent to harm.
- Theft, fraud or forgery.
- Habitual drunkenness or drunk driving.
- Illegal gambling.
- Prostitution.
- Any offense that involves perjury or false statements.

- Offenses against a person because of race, religion, national origin, political opinion or social group (i.e. hate crimes).

YOUR RECORD

Remember when you were arrested late one night outside the Whataburger for – what was it? – public intoxication, assault, minor in possession? You don't even really remember what happened to the case. Who knows? It may be on your "record." Hell, what is a record these days?

Criminal records. In the old days before computers, a person's "record" referred to their "rap sheet." The records relating to convictions and arrests were not readily accessible to the public because of the nature of keeping records. A background check was an extremely time-intensive search of county and state records.

These days, if you have been arrested and charged with a crime, records relating to your arrest and identifying information are entered throughout the criminal justice system in huge computer databases.

Imagine the flow of information. The arresting agency, say the Houston Police Department, enters your name into its computers. Upon arriving at the jail, the record of your arrest is entered into the jail records; photographs and fingerprints are taken and sent to the Texas Department of Public Safety and a national database. DPS can also forward these records to federal law enforcement agencies. If you were interviewed by Harris County Pre-Trial Services for release on personal bond, your information will be entered in its computer. The county and district clerk, as well as the district attorney's office, will open files and enter your information into their computers. If the arrest involved a driver's license suspension – whether ultimately suspended or not – Texas DPS will make those notations in your driving record. Not only is the traditional paper trail growing, but the "digital" trail grows exponentially. Criminal records are maintained by the Texas Department of Public Safety in the Texas Crime Information Computer and the Federal Bureau of Investigations in its National Crime Information Computer. These agencies' record databases are not open to the public, but law enforcement and prosecutorial offices can check these records any time they like. The general public has full access to files in all district and county clerk's offices in the state of Texas, but not these.

Many people have the misconception that if their case was dismissed, the records no longer exist. If you have been arrested and charged with a crime, getting the case dismissed does not mean that the records disappear. Granted, a "criminal record" does not exist, but any and all entities that made a record of your arrest retain those records, unless a court orders the destruction of those records.

The county or district clerk's office or the municipal court where you were charged has a file concerning the incident. These files are public information. That means banks, credit services and future employers or anyone else who wants to search your records can do so. The accessibility to these records becomes easier as more and more of these records are computerized. Anyone can discover prior criminal conduct by simply searching for your name at the county courthouse or municipal court (or even online if they know where to search). More and more companies use these background searches as screening tools of potential employees. The record of the arrest, the offense report, fingerprints, case disposition, etc. are still around unless you act to expunge those records.

Do I have a criminal record? If you think you may have a record of an arrest or conviction, you can check your criminal history by mail or in person from the Texas Department of Public Safety. A written request for the Criminal History Record Information must be submitted along with:

- Printed name of the individual. Include any other names used. (Order of names: last, middle, first), sex, race, date of birth.
- A complete and legible set of fingerprints on a DPS approved

fingerprint card taken by a law enforcement officer. (Most local police and sheriff's departments will provide this service and may charge a fee (often $5). However, it is the responsibility of the individual to mail or bring the completed card to Austin, along with the other necessary information. If you go to DPS in Austin, workers will fingerprint you and run the CHRI for $15. It takes between 2-4 hours.
- Social Security number.
- Return address and phone number of the individual or authorized representative.
- Cash, check or U.S. money order for $15 per each fingerprint card.

Mail the written request and the fingerprint card with payment to:

Texas Department of Public Safety
Crime Records Service
P.O. Box 15999
Austin, Texas 78761-5999
Attention: Correspondence Supervisor

If a criminal history record is found, it along with the original fingerprint card will be returned; if no record is found, the fingerprint card will be returned with a notation indicating no criminal record.

Cleaning up your record: Expunction. A process known as expunction is the only way that records of arrest and prosecution can be removed. The process involves filing a civil lawsuit against all departments and entities that maintain those records to expunge or destroy the records. Generally, if a misdemeanor has been dismissed or acquitted by the judge or a jury, then expunction is available. An expunction is also available if a felony has been dismissed before being presented to a grand jury, acquitted by a judge or a jury, or dismissed and the statute of limitations has run. It also might be available if the case was presented to a grand jury based upon mistake or false information.

Finally, the person seeking expunction must not been convicted of a felony in the five years preceding the date of the arrest.

To have your records expunged, a petition for expunction must be filed in the district court of the county where you were arrested; all parties retaining records must be named and served; and the petition must be presented to the court for ruling. Once the court determines that you qualify, it orders all agencies to destroy the records related to your arrest. It is as if the arrest never occurred.

Legal effect of expunction. The release, dissemination, or use of the expunged records and files for any purpose is prohibited. You may deny the occurrence of the arrest and the existence of the expunction order, with the exception of the following: you or any other person, when questioned under oath in a criminal proceeding about an arrest for which the records have been expunged, may state only that the matter in question has been expunged.

Non-disclosure of records and deferred adjudication. Unfortunately, many people are erroneously told that deferred adjudication will result in no "criminal record" and the case will be dismissed after you successfully serve the probation period. This is partially correct. While the case is dismissed, the records of the arrest, prosecution and deferred adjudication remain for all to see.

If you are placed on court-ordered supervision, you are not entitled to have your records expunged. Successfully completing a term of deferred adjudication does not result in a conviction, but your criminal history will always show that you were arrested, charged and the case was dismissed. A deferred adjudication that qualifies under certain legal guidelines can be sealed from public dissemination, but, like expunction, this too requires petitioning the court of supervision and other legal requirements.

A petition for non-disclosure may be filed upon the dismissal or discharge in most misdemeanor cases, except those involving assault, kidnapping, unlawful restraint, sexual offenses, disorderly conduction, weapons violations and offenses against the family.

In those cases, a person must wait five years after dismissal or discharge to file a petition; and ten years following discharge or dismissal in all qualified felonies.

There are other limitations such as anyone who has been convicted or placed on deferred adjudication does not qualify or those who have been placed on deferred adjudication for an offense (except transportation code violations punishable by fine only) during the applicable time periods above.

Other limitations may also arise, as the Texas Legislature continues to tinker with this statute and will probably continue to do so. If you are interested in exploring the possibility or are worried about a record of arrest, charge or conviction, consult with a reputable attorney for more particular advice.

Juvenile records. Everyone seems to think that once you turn 18 your record is somehow wiped clean and you start over. This is not the case. Generally speaking, convictions while a minor cannot be used to enhance punishment of "adult" offenses. However, in some instances it can be considered at punishment and any offense that relates to alcohol, tobacco or drugs can be used to elevate the seriousness of subsequent offenses.

"IT WASN'T ME, IT WAS HIM"

It's late and the bars have closed, and no place will sell you beer, but you and your buddies aren't quite ready to call it a night. Y'all jokingly talk about stealing some beer from the convenience store, but y'all all laugh and forget about it. Your buddy Joe asks you to stop at the store so he can buy some cigarettes. You stop and wait for him to go in. All of a sudden, Joe runs out of the store with two cases of beer under his arms, and jumps in the car yelling, "Go, go, go!!!" and you speed off.

Although you are plenty pissed off at your friend, you get over it as y'all finish off the case of beer he snagged from the store. The next day a knock at the door reveals a police officer and BANG, you are arrested for theft. How can that be if you really didn't do anything but drive off after Joe had already stolen the beer?

Parties to a crime. You may be criminally responsible for an offense committed by someone else if you promoted or assisted in the commission of the offense.

In the situation above, you aided in the theft and flight from by driving the getaway car.

You have probably seen on the news where two guys go into a store to rob the place and one of them shoots the clerk. Both robbers most likely were charged with the capital murder, because it was reasonably foreseeable that in the course of a robbery someone may get hurt or even killed, even if the other guy didn't even known the shooter had a gun.

Conspiracy. On a boring Friday night, you and some of the guys hatch a plan to steal some beer from the country club. One of you used to work there, so you know that the club keeps beer and liquor in a storage locker. You plan the caper, and each of you has a role to play. One of you will drive; one is gonna get out and cut the lock and the other two will go in and get the booze and load it in the trunk. BANG, a conspiracy is born: conspiracy to commit the offense of burglary of a building.

All that needs to happen to complete the crime is one of you to do anything in furtherance of the agreement. All of you getting in the car with the tools to break the lock and starting out will probably do it, even if you get to the country club and you decide that this is really not such a good idea.

Conspiracy is rarely prosecuted in Texas. The next section covers the more popular offense prosecuted in these types of situation.

Organized criminal activity. A person commits an offense if he establishes, maintains, or participates or in the profits as a member of a criminal street gang or he commits or conspires to commit one or more of the specific crimes listed under this section of the penal code, which are numerous.

Once a person is involved in an organized criminal activity the only way out is a voluntary and complete rejection of his criminal objective by withdrawing before the crime is committed and taking action to prevent the offense.

"I DIDN'T REALLY DO ANYTHING"

Attempted crimes. Criminal attempt is committed if a person intends to commit a crime but fails to carry out the offense (but goes further than mere preparation). An attempted offense is one category lower than the offense attempted.

ARREST AND BAIL

You find yourself being asked to place your hands behind your back and are being taken into custody. You are under arrest. You are placed in the back seat of a patrol car and BANG, you're going to jail. Hopefully, you did not skip right to this section and read the earlier section regarding dealing with the police.

You have a constitutional right to be released on reasonable bond. Upon arrest, a person is initially taken to the jail of the arresting agency and must, without unnecessary delay, be taken before a magistrate. Anyone who is arrested — if not released by the arresting agency — is eventually "booked" into jail and taken before a magistrate. At that appearance, the magistrate must inform the accused of his constitutional rights and determine whether probable cause exists for the arrest and whether a bond should be set. This procedure usually occurs within 24 hours of the arrest. Do not plead "guilty" to the charge in front of the magistrate unless you are completely certain that is what you want to do because it will result in a conviction and remain on your criminal record.

You will normally be given an opportunity to make a phone call, but again, this is reality and not TV. You don't get one phone call by right. Remain courteous. Being rude and obnoxious will not help in your defense and may get you beaten or thrown into an very unpleasant place or in a cell with Bruno, the 6-foot-5 cross-dresser who just threw up himself and is in a very amorous or angry mood.

If and when you do get access to a phone, call someone you know will answer and accept a collect call. If your roommate answers, tell him quickly and calmly that he needs to find this book and read about bail, then scrape together some money and get you out or call your parents. Never discuss the facts of the arrest or the charge with anyone except your attorney and never over the jail phone. These phones are monitored and recorded, as are conversations in the cells, visitation areas, and rooms of the jail.

In most counties, bonds are usually based on bond schedule that sets a standard bail amount for the various crimes. Under certain circumstances, bond may be denied. A judge may set bail, reduce it or even the bail amount depending on the circumstances.

There are three ways to be released on bond:

- Post a cash bond in the full amount. If the person on bond appears as directed the cash bond will be returned once the case has been resolved, usually within six to twelve weeks.
- Hire a professional bondsman, who will charge a fee, usually between five and twenty percent of the bond, depending on the circumstances and the collateral. The bondsman has an agreement with the county to guarantee the appearance of the accused at all court ordered appearances; otherwise, the bond is forfeited and the bondsman is responsible for the entire amount of the bond.
- Most larger counties in Texas have a pretrial service agency that administers the pretrial release of accused citizens. Based upon an interview and the recommendations of the agency, a judge will decide whether to grant a pretrial bond. Release in this manner is far less expensive. However, the agency will likely require more effort and conditions than a bonding company.

Once your roommate has scurried around all morning trying to spring you from the slammer, you are finally released "on bond." First things first, go home and take a shower. Second, take your roommate out to breakfast. No matter how awful an experience your night in the slammer was, his was equally frustrating and unpleasant dealing with the bureaucracy of the authorities trying to get you out.

In the worst-case scenario, your roommate couldn't get you out because your case said "no bond." This designation means the accused will not be released and happens under the following conditions:

- The accused is on probation or on bond for a felony.
- He is charged with a crime of violence.
- He has previously been sentenced to prison two or more times.
- He has been arrested on a parole violation.

Unless one of these situations apply, don't freak out. A "no bond" designation does not always mean that the person will not get a bond set, but you will most likely have to wait until you are taken before a judge. Your attorney should approach the judge to request that reasonable bond be set.

I think I have a warrant. You pick up your date one Friday night. On the way to the party, you roll through a stop sign and after the cop runs your license, he asks you to step out of the car. You have a warrant and BANG. The speeding ticket you got last spring break escaped your memory. Instead of real funky love action after the party, you get to spend the night with all the other losers in the holdover cell.

Like we talked about earlier, warrants usually come back to bite you in the ass at a really inconvenient time. If you think you have a warrant out for your arrest, contact the local law enforcement agencies that may have a record of your warrant and ask if they would run your identifying information to confirm the warrant. Don't worry, they are not going to trace your call and come arrest you, unless, of course, you are really wanted. They actually want you to clear the warrant and will usually give you whatever information you need to clear it. If not, call a lawyer or bondsman. If you have a warrant, you have four basic choices:

- Wait until a law enforcement officer takes you to jail.
- Turn yourself in to the local jail.
- Pay the full amount of the bond (i.e. cash bond).
- Post a bond with a bail bond agency.

Collect up your money and go make the bond. Don't take the risk of losing your job or being embarrassed in front of your family, friends or co-workers, or hell, even in class.

ANATOMY OF A CRIMINAL TRIAL

Voir dire: Otherwise known as jury selection or, rather, de-selection. The first six (misdemeanor) or twelve (felony) juror candidates who are not struck make up the jury.

Opening statements: Attorneys give the jury a broad overview of what evidence they expect to be presented, setting the stage for the trial.

Presentation of evidence: Exhibits introduced into evidence and the testimony of witnesses are the evidence. The state goes first. After a witness is called by one side, the other gets to cross-examine him. The defense does not have to present any evidence or witnesses and may rest after the state's presentation.

Witnesses: The jury decides the credibility of the witness and can accept or reject all or part of any witnesses' testimony for any reason, but it must start each witness at the same level of creditability before he ever says a word.

Closing arguments: Lawyers for each side are allowed to summarize the evidence to try to persuade the jury to accept their view of the case. It is not evidence, just the lawyer's view of the evidence.

Jury deliberations and decision: After closing arguments, the jury is sent to deliberate and can only consider the evidence they heard at trial. The jury will decide if the state proved its case beyond a reasonable doubt and decide by a unanimous verdict of either guilty or not guilty.

THE OTHER SIDE – THE COMPLAINING WITNESS

We have been talking about the accused quite a lot and it is just as important that any citizen who feels he has been wronged has the right to bring that person or entity into court to answer for their actions. In civil matters it is usually a question of money or divorce, but if the person feels that it is criminal act, he can simply swear out complaints and aid the state in charging and prosecuting the case.

Filing charges. Contact the local law enforcement office and make a formal report or complaint, but do not try to use the system as leverage or intimidation. Whenever you report a crime, be accurate and truthful at all times, otherwise you may subject yourself to criminal prosecution.

Victims' rights. There are specific rights associated with those who have been victims of crime. If you have been the victim of sexual assault, kidnapping or aggravated robbery or if you have suffered bodily injury as the result of a crime, or if you are the close relative or guardian of a deceased victim, you have the right to:

- Be protected from harm or threats.
- Information about the defendant's right to bail and to have your safety considered in the setting of bail.
- Information about court proceedings, if you so request, and to be present at all public proceedings subject to the approval of the judge.
- Information about stages in the criminal justice system in general, including criminal investigations, trials, plea bargaining, appeals and parole.
- Provide information to the probation department concerning the impact of the crime for inclusion in the pre-sentence investigation report to the judge, and to complete a victim impact statement.
- Information regarding compensation to crime victims under

the Crime Victims' Compensation Act, payment for a medical examination for a victim of sexual assault and referral to available social service agencies that may offer additional assistance.

- Notification, if requested, of any parole proceedings regarding the defendant, and the right to participate in those proceedings.
- A waiting area in the courthouse separate from the defendant and his or her family and witnesses, or if a separate area is not possible, to have safeguards to ensure minimal contact.
- Prompt return of property held by law enforcement or the attorney for the state after the property is no longer needed as evidence;
- Notification to your employer by the prosecuting attorney, if you must be absent from work in order to be in court or to otherwise cooperate in the case.

Protective orders. A citizen may request the county or district attorney's office to protect family members and individuals involved in a dating relationship at no cost. The citizen will have to fill out and execute a sworn affidavit that sets out the facts supporting that violence has occurred and is likely to occur in the future. Once a complaint is filed and the affidavit is received, an application for a protective order and temporary protective order will be filed and presented to a district judge. The judge will review the application and affidavit and, if sufficient evidence exists, will sign and enter the temporary protective order and set a hearing within 14 days. The respondent will then be served and noticed to be at the hearing.

Both parties normally appear at the hearing, with a permanent protective order being entered. The protective order can be up to two years and can require alcohol, drug and anger counseling. The court may also prohibit or order either party to or not do any number of things involving counseling, places they cannot go, people they cannot contact, possession of property, including forbidding them access to their children and homes.

CHAPTER 4
SEX, RELATIONSHIPS, AND RELATED ISSUES

THE HOOK-UP

WHETHER IT'S AN OLD-SCHOOL "blind date," "fix-up" or "one night stand," or a more modern digital app that makes these meetings happen, they can all lead to "the hook-up."

Sex. Our society has failed to adequately socialize boys and girls about how to treat the opposite sex and what is and is not acceptable behavior. This has led to some common "mis-beliefs" by both sexes. Generally speaking, men view women as either virtuous or sexually "loose," so they're confused when it comes to understanding or interpreting the sexual desires of the women. A common "misbelief" girls have is that young men are more knowledgeable about sex and thus, they should defer to their lead; and, men usually interpret flirtatious behavior as being led on, giving them the green light to become more forward or aggressive.

Uncertainties and "misbeliefs" go uncorrected or are not clarified because both sexes remain reluctant to express their feelings with the other sex. Even when their physical behavior, such as crying, slamming doors and rolled eyes prompt the question, "Whats wrong?," the response is usually "nothing." The response doesn't match the physical behavior, thus confusing the other person. This "confusion" and lack of communication spills over into sexual situations, contributing to both sexes' confusion in trying to decipher the other's actions and words.

The basic lesson to be learned: "Say what you mean and mean what you say." Do not be afraid to express yourself. It will reduce the risk of misunderstanding, embarrassment and humiliation in those uncomfortable situations that have progressed to the point that no other option seems possible. This will also spill over into other aspects of personal relationships and create more free and fulfilling sexual relationships.

Having sex is about making choices and comes with responsibilities and even possible life-changing results. One of the great joys of life can be having a baby — when you are ready and are able to provide the love, care and support a child needs. One of the great setbacks in life can be an unintended pregnancy — especially for a young woman. Unless you want to risk a pregnancy, take some precautions and use contraception, not to mention to may also avoid a nasty sexually transmitted disease) like herpes, chlamydia, gonorrhea, HPV, or even HIV/AIDS.

The digital hookup and bad people. Digital conveniences can be a prime tool for those looking to rob, rape or take advantage of someone. Do not put yourself in a vulnerable position and be cautious of anything that sounds too good to be true.

How old is old enough? In Texas, when you turn 17, you are no longer considered a "child," according to the Texas Penal Code, and are considered old enough to lawfully engage in consensual sex as long as certain age limitations are followed. Anyone who engages in even consensual sex with someone under seventeen may face criminal charges with certain exceptions. If one person is under seventeen, any consensual sexual conduct or exposure with someone more than three years older is unlawful. Therefore, if you are about to engage in consensual sexual acts with someone between 14 and 17, and you are more than three years older than that person, you better think twice and consider waiting until that person turns 17 or find another date. Otherwise, you face a charge of sexual assault, which is second degree felony and can be prosecuted up to 10 years after the victim turns eighteen. One other reminder, it doesn't matter if she told you she was old enough or that she is the one of the biggest sluts you've ever seen. If she is below 14, it becomes an aggravated crime, a first degree felony.

Deviate sex. Texas has made it a crime for anyone to engage in "deviate sexual intercourse" with anyone. The definition of "deviate sexual intercourse" in Texas is any contact between any part of the genitals of one person and the mouth or anus of another person; or the penetration of the genitals or the anus of another person with an object, including a finger. Under a strict interpretation of this law, oral sex is considered to be deviate sexual conduct, but not illegal in and of itself, unless done so in conjunction with certain other circumstances,.

Public sex. It's a nice afternoon and Joe decides to go to the park with his girlfriend. They find a nice out-of-the-way spot among the trees, have a nice picnic and couple of beers when Joe's girlfriend starts to get a little more amorous. Joe and his girl undress each other and roll around in the grass having sex in various ways and means. Two kids wander out of the nearby woods and witness Joe's sexual prowess, not to mention their full frontal nudity. The kids, after standing there and gawking, inform their parents on the other side of the park, who in turn summon the park police. BANG, no pun intended, Joe and his love may be subject to arrest and prosecution for several different offenses, such as public lewdness and indecent exposure.

Public lewdness occurs when someone engages in a sexual act in a public place or, if not in a public place, is reckless about whether another is present and will be offended or alarmed by the behavior. This could include activities inside a person's home or on their own property if it is done so in a reckless manner (i.e. can someone see it?). So be careful with the car and elevator sex.

Indecency with a child is the most serious of these three potential problems for Joe and his nature-loving girl, albeit unlikely unless other more aggravating circumstances arose.

Unable to consent, "like a dead fish." Let's say Joe has been out at a fraternity party and he meets a girl, and they have some drinks, dance, talk, laugh, and have more drinks. They really hit it off, but she has had a little too much to drink or may even be under the influence of a drug (prescription or otherwise). She and Joe are having a good time, mugging down in the corner and getting pretty hardcore. During the evening, Joe has even had the opportunity to see her license and his concerns raised by the above section are put to rest. Joe offers to make sure she gets home safely, but when they get there, she asks Joe in. She turns on the TV and, while sitting on the couch, they start kissing. Things progress and she even takes her shirt and jeans off. She's totally naked, but then proceeds to pass out. Not knowing what to do, Joe decides to go on without her and engages in sexual conduct with her, even though she is passed out like a "dead fish." Under the sexual assault provision of the Texas Penal Code, it is considered an offense if the person has not consented AND the other person knows that he or she is unconscious or physically unable to resist. If you find yourself in Joe's shoes, be a gentleman, make her comfortable, cover her up, lock the door and go home. Call her the next morning or leave her a nice note with your number.

Other legal ramifications may arise if you happen to provide your sexual partner with some popular forms of drugs such as ecstasy, GHB, Rohypnol, ketamine and others, especially if she isn't aware of your "practical joke." It's no joke and raises the offense to "aggravated" status.

No means no. One last word on this topic that hopefully goes without saying: "NO MEANS NO." Any hint of conduct without consent or remorse or guilt after the fact is precarious ground that can easily result in charges being accepted by the district attorney. Regret, embarrassment and humiliation have all been common motivations for false allegations the next morning and nothing will totally prevent you being accused of something criminal, but remember that taking advantage, coercing, or humiliating someone can all approach the line that can easily be interpreted as being without consent. If you try to conduct yourself as a gentleman, you will most likely avoid any allegation of misconduct and have all the fun in the world.

Date rape. Every young woman should be conscious of date rape and protecting herself from a situation in which she has no control. It is a serious crime and can occur just as easily in casual as well as serious relationships.

Pickup or date rape? It is important for me to stress that what I am going to relate is drawn from numerous sources and merely overgeneralizes possible situations. This is intended to give you information to protect yourself and help assess any number of situations. I also want to stress that if you are interested in engaging in intimate relations with someone or even just trying to get to know some guy you just met, don't immediately suspect that a clumsy, awkward or rude date is some sort of sexual predator. Evaluate the situation and try to remove yourself from the situation if uncomfortable or alarming and always try not to put yourself in a vulnerable situation, unless you are comfortable with what is going on.

You are at a frat party or a loud dance club having some drinks with friends and doing the things that college girls do. A couple of guys come by and y'all strike up a conversation. He's cute so you and he get closer to talk over the loud music. He puts his hand on your knee, but you don't say anything and continue to talk and maybe even flirt a little. He then brushes against you or even puts his hand on your butt. Again, you don't say anything about his "roaming hands." You then suggest that y'all go someplace less crowded.

Date rape interpretation: You are the target of a typical date rapist. He chooses to be in the crowded and loud party to get close to you. Placing his hand on your knee is his attempt at invading and testing your personal space. Without any objection to his actions, he proceeds to the second stage in which he attempts to desensitize you to the intrusion by escalating the behavior (moving his hands to your butt, for example). It's unlikely that you tell him that you are uncomfortable with his "roaming hands" but you also feel uneasy with his behavior and suggest going someplace less crowded, because you don't want your friends to see how forward he is being or you really don't want to stay close to him. He misinterprets your suggestion as your way to be alone with him. When y'all are in an isolated place, the rapist attacks.

Pick-up interpretation: You are part of the age-old ritual of the pick-up. He chooses to be in the crowded bar or loud party to meet women. He placed his hand on your knee to make the first move and gauge his chances. Without objection or even a witty remark objecting, he gets a little more friendly. Again, without any objection or sign of displeasure, he perceives you as receptive to his advances. Your suggestion of going someplace less crowded is definitely interpreted as receptive to more advances and when y'all are in an isolated place, y'all have a very nice time together or you finally tell him that you are not ready to "get it on" just yet.

If you do not want to go down the road toward a sexual encounter, don't put yourself in a position to be taken advantage of. If you are not interested, don't let him control the situation. If he does something that makes you uncomfortable, be polite and point out his indiscretion, more than once if necessary. Whether an awkward pick-up or potential rapist, calling attention to any inappropriate behavior or unwanted advances may prevent a bad situation at the start, but if he continues to be aggressive, it should signal to you that it may be more than just the pick-up and it should send up the red flag. No matter which is the case, you should never separate yourself from your friends or a crowded place. Passivity will always be perceived as condoning whatever sexual advances that are being made toward you. Lastly, confidence, provocativeness, and flirtation can sometimes be interpreted as being receptive to a man's sexual advances. I am certainly not advocating doubles-standards. I am simply suggesting that women should be aware of how their behavior be perceived.

Date rape drugs: Alcohol and drugs are often involved in incidents of acquaintance or date rape. A study of rape in Canada suggested that alcohol was used by half of all offenders and a third of the victims. Date rape drugs are often slipped into a victim's drink. These drugs, as well as alcohol, can make a person unable to resist assault, and even suffer a type of amnesia, so the "victim" is uncertain about what happened.

I want to stop here and preach a little.

Just because you got drunk and had sex with someone or everyone in the living room of the frat house does not mean that you have been sexually assaulted. Just because you are embarrassed by your actions, even if you took some type of drug someone gave you and you are now having trouble remembering the night's events and just because you don't remember this event until the pictures appear around campus or on the Internet, still doesn't mean that you have been the victim of sexual assault. You just had bad judgment that night. It is when you are unaware that you took the drug or were tricked into it and then taken advantage of during a state of impairment that you may be a victim of a sexual assault. Likewise, even if you did overindulge, passed out and were then taken advantage of, this too may be a sexual assault. Know what you are doing and always be prepared for the consequences; embarrassment or humiliation later does not make a sexual act a sexual assault. It is when it is without your consent at the time of the act that makes it illegal. Have a good time, but at least be aware of what you're drinking or taking and try to make judgments that you are prepared to accept.

Always be wary about accepting drinks from anyone you don't know well or long enough to trust. If you do accept a drink, make sure it's from an unopened container, one that you open yourself and don't put your drink down and leave it unattended, even to go to the restroom.

The so-called "date rape drugs" are illegal to possess without prescription and usually have no color, smell, or taste and are easily added to drinks without anyone knowing. These drugs usually cause a person to become incapacitated and physically unable to protect themselves and not even remember the event. These drugs are suspected to cause health problems and, in some cases, may even cause death.

Rohypnol: Generically called flunitrazepam, it is prescribed as a sleeping pill outside of the United States and is used as a short-term treatment for insomnia, as a sedative hypnotic and a pre-anesthetic.

Street names: rophies, roofies, R2, roofenol, Roche, roachies, la rocha, rope, rib, circles, Mexican valium, roach-2, roopies, forget-me pill, trip & fall, mind erasers and ropies.

Looks like: White tablet, scored on one side, with the word ROCHE and an encircled "one" or "two" (depending on the dosage) on the other. They are sold in pre-sealed bubble packs of one or two mg doses. Rohypnol can often be dissolved in a drink. Newer pills turn blue in liquid.

Ketamine: This liquid is used to anesthetize animals. It can be made into a tablet or a powder by evaporating the liquid and reducing it to a fine white powder that can be smoked or snorted. Some reports indicate it is sometimes sold as MDMA (Ecstasy) and mixed with other drugs such as ephedrine and caffeine.

Street names: K, Ket, Special K, Vitamin K, Vit K, Kit Kat, Keller, Kelly's day, Green, Blind squid, Cat valium, Purple, Special la coke, Super acid, and Super C.

Looks like: Clear liquid or a white powder, which is often mistaken for cocaine or crystal methamphetamine.

GHB (gamma-hydroxybutrate): Originally used in psychiatric treatments, this has been abused in the U.S. for euphoric, sedative and anabolic (bodybuilding) effects.

Street names: G, Georgia Home Boy, Liquid Ecstasy, Grievous Bodily Harm, Liquid E, GBH, Soap, Scoop, Easy Lay, Salty Water, G-Riffick, Cherry Meth, Nature's Quaalude, Zonked, Organic Quaalude, Somatomax, G, Jib, Woman's Viagra, Gamma 10, GH Buddy, Aminos, Blue Nitro, Blue Thunder, Thunder Nectar, Renewtrient, Revivarant, Remforce, Firewater, and Invigorate.

Looks like: Clear liquid with no odor or color or white powder.

"I can't remember what happened. I think I was drugged." If you suspect that you have been drugged without your knowledge, whether you think you were sexually assaulted or not, you should seek to have toxicology screen immediately. Popular "date rape" drugs are eliminated from the body quickly and there is a small window to detect their presence. Don't hesitate, it may preserve evidence that is important later. Go to a hospital or clinic and request a drug/tox screen and have blood drawn immediately that can be preserved for testing.

THE SERIOUS RELATIONSHIP

The "hook-up" can often develop into a regular dating relationship. When that happens, it is also common for the two of you to spend more time together. Whether it's "FBO" (Facebook official) or you're still just "talking," "hanging," "messing around," or just consider yourselves FWB, the state of Texas considers y'all to be in a "dating relationship." This is a relationship between individuals who have or have had a continuing relationship of a romantic or intimate nature. The existence of such a relationship shall be determined based on the length of the relationship, the nature of the relationship and the frequency and type of interaction between the persons involved in the relationship. The law also notes that a "casual acquaintanceship or ordinary fraternization in a business or social context does not constitute a 'dating relationship,' " but can also include a present or past "romantic" relationship.

Since you are now "dating," the law considers you both to be on the same level as a spouse, family or household member.

This comes with the raised expectations that you treat each other with greater respect and are now to avoid any assaultive behavior towards each other. Anything of that nature is now considered "domestic" or "family" violence and comes with more harsh punishments.

Living together. You find yourself spending all your time together, spending the nights together, maybe even abandoning one of your places for the convenience of the other's. You keep a toothbrush, clothes, and a few other personal effects there. Things are getting serious and then one of you maybe suggests something to the effect that it simply makes sense to live together. Congratulations on taking this step, but be mindful that while it seems that this eases many complications, it comes with its own separate and new complications to deal with, but that is beyond the scope of this book.

Almost everything in Chapter 10 is applicable here regarding legal responsibilities relating to the contractual aspects of leases, utilities and living arrangements. While each of you may not see yourselves as anything other than "roommates with benefits" and have no intention toward marriage, the law can view this relationship more than just a convenient living arrangement. If that is the case, make sure you do not blur those lines.

Common-law marriage. In Texas there is something called a "common law marriage." A valid common law marriage requires the following:

- Agree to be married. This is an important factor that requires both parties to have the intent or desire to live as if formally married.
- Cohabitate in Texas as husband and wife. Something a little more than just having sexual relations while living under the same roof and it does not have to be continuous, but without evidence to the contrary, living together can be evidence of marriage.
- The couple hold themselves out as married. Basically telling other people that you're married (even just once) does it. Introducing yourselves as married or doing something that makes

people think you're married, like joint credit applications or naming the other as his or her spouse on a life insurance policy, including the other on insurance or an apartment lease. Purchasing property or getting a mortgage or loan is also a significant act that suggests a marriage exists.

Some simple steps will help ensure that you remain single until you're ready for marriage. The simple lesson here is that unless you absolutely intend to go forward as married, don't do anything that suggests otherwise. Make sure your landlord understands that you are not married and that you are simply tenants in common on the lease. Sign any documents carefully and make sure nothing in the document suggests a marital relationship and sign as an individual. File your taxes separately and avoid joint bank or credit accounts and don't use each other's last names. Make sure your social media accounts don't indicate that your status is "married" and don't post anything that would suggest your partner is a husband or wife or that you are married. Sound farfetched? Trust me, it's not and it happens.

Once a marriage is established, whether formally with a license or common law, the other is entitled to half of your common property. It can become quite complex if there are any assets, so simply don't put yourself in that position until you are absolutely sure you want to be married.

Domestic violence and abusive relationships. No matter your gender, if you've suffered abuse, it is important to understand that you are not at fault and you did not cause the abuse to occur. You are not responsible for the violent behavior of someone else. Try to identify potential problems and takes steps to avoid future problems and situations. Always protect yourself.

Signs of abuse. It may be embarrassing, difficult and confusing to admit that you are in an abusive relationship or to find a way out, but signs indicating abuse or a potential for abuse include:

- Keeping track of what you are doing all the time and criticizing you for little things.

- Constantly accusing you of being unfaithful.
- Preventing or discouraging you from seeing friends or family, or going to work or school.
- Getting angry when drinking alcohol or using drugs.
- Controlling all the money you spend.
- Humiliating you in front of others.
- Destroying your property or things that you care about.
- Threatening to hurt you or the children or pets, or causing harm (by hitting, punching, slapping, kicking, or biting).
- Using or threatening to use a weapon against you.
- Forcing you to have sex against your will.
- Blaming you for his/her violent outbursts.

I've been physically abused. Things you can do include:

- Leave immediately, especially if you or your children are in danger!
- Call a crisis hotline or the National Domestic Violence Hotline 800-799-SAFE or TDD 800-787-3224, which is available 24-7, in English, Spanish, and other languages and will give you the phone numbers of local hotlines and other resources.
- Understand that you're not alone. Anyone can be a victim of domestic abuse.
- Don't ignore it or wait for it to go away. It won't go away.
- Don't keep it to yourself. Get help and talk with someone: a family member, friend, colleague, or faith counselor.
- If you've been hurt, get medical attention and call the police and take pictures of the injuries.

THE BREAK-UP (TALES OF THE CRAZY EX)

All of us have had relationships end. Some are congenial, while others are acrimonious and seem to never end. Relationships are hard and can impact our lives far beyond the relationship itself.

The following sections are written using an androgynous name for our boy/girlfriend, Finn, or you can insert the appropriate name to customize each section for your own cray-cray ex. Each story should help illustrate the need to understand that your or your date's behavior could have consequences, so cool down and think before you act.

Assaultive conduct: Finn had a temper, commonly known as a short fuse and sometimes you never knew what would set it off. Several times Finn had either initiated or reacted with physical or abusive conduct. Such situations included yelling at the meter maid after she issued a parking ticket, threatening to kick some guy's ass for sneaking a parking space, (Class C misdemeanors), yelling threatening insults at an umpire at Finn's nephew's little league game (Class B misdemeanor), "bitch-slapping" a doorman at a club (Class A misdemeanor), smacking a brother for an embarrassing comment in front of friends at the movies (third degree felony), hitting a cop in the head while struggling during an arrest for protesting (third degree felony), and whacking me in the shin with a broom stick, requiring nine stitches (second degree felony). Not that Finn was charged in each of these offenses, but certainly an arrest and charge may have been warranted.

Breaking the news: Over and above the obvious signs, the biggest problem was Finn's unhealthy neediness, not to mention there were indications that Finn was unfaithful. Thus, there was trouble in paradise and you had to end it. Finn did not take the news well. Finn slaps you across the face and then starts wrecking the apartment. You tell Finn to calm down and stop trashing the place or you'll call the cops. In response, Finn grabs the phone and throws it out the window. That's interference with an emergency telephone call. Finn knowingly prevented and interfered with your ability to place an emergency telephone call and recklessly rendered unusable the telephone that would otherwise be used to request assistance in an emergency. Finn committed a Class A misdemeanor, except that the offense is a state jail felony if she has been convicted for this before. This may also be an assault for Finn smacking you in the face and criminal mischief if there was damage to the phone or the apartment.

A helpful suggestion is that this conversation should be had when others are close at hand or in a public place to diffuse the situation and hopefully create witnesses, should there be allegations that you did something wrong.

Finn threatens to get you: As Finn flails around the apartment throwing and breaking most of your stuff, as well as the phone, Finn whacks herself with the phone right in the side of the face. It leaves a nice mark and everyone who witnessed Finn's rampage finds it humorous. As she storms out, Finn threatens to "get" you. Everyone else leaves and you began to clean up the apartment. A few minutes later, there's a knock on the door. Two police officers inform you that Finn had called the cops and claimed not only that you had hit her in the face, but also that she was living with you and you had done it on numerous times before. The cops see the mess. You try to explain that it was her that went nuts, but she made the call, was quite convincing, had an injury consistent with the allegation and, well, she was small, cute and crying. They don't really listen to anything you say and BANG, they take you to jail for assault on a family member, domestic violence. Normally, a person is charged with a Class A misdemeanor if someone claims that he intentionally, knowingly, or recklessly caused them bodily injury. It's a third degree felony if the offense is committed against a public servant, member of the defendant's family or household or if he has been convicted of an offense against a member of the defendant's family.

By the way, "family" includes individuals related, including former spouses, dating relationships, parents of the same child, whether those individuals reside together or not and "household" means a unit composed of persons living together in the same dwelling, without regard to whether they are related to each other. This also includes roommates and live-in girlfriends.

It took a good attorney and some time to get the D.A. to finally see the light and understand that you weren't a woman beater. The charge was finally dismissed but it was not easy or inexpensive, not to mention the cost of getting the record expunged.

Finn's a liar: In an unusual situation, the D.A. sees through her evil and manipulative ways and actually charges her with making a false report for her rampage. This does not usually occur, but her actions and situation warrant such a charge, because when she called the cops and reported that you had assaulted her, she intended to deceive by making a false statement that was material to a criminal investigation to a peace officer conducting the investigation.

The breakup continues: With all this going on, you go out to the parking lot to find a nice long, deep scratch running the length of the car. Clearly, someone has left you a message. No evidence of who it was, but you know Finn or someone left you a gift. The severity of the offense depends on the amount of monetary damage, ranging from less than $50 for a Class C misdemeanor to $200,000 or more for a first-degree felony.

Finn's not gonna let go: Finn is not taking the separation well. His jealousy and domineering personality cannot seem to let you go, so begin the endless silent phone calls, hang-ups and abusive, obscene emails, social media posts and threatening texts. It's harassment. Finn clearly intends to harass, annoy, alarm, abuse, torment, or embarrass you and has done so in several ways that constitute a Class B misdemeanor offense.

Now Finn's a stalker: It's getting out of control and Finn can be found every single time you leave you class or hang out at your apartment's pool. It is clear that Finn was following you around. You feel threatened by this. Then you find a note on your door suggesting that some unfortunate accident would soon befall you, your mother, your dog "Sparky," and maybe even the stray cat you feed on the patio. BANG, you're being stalked, a third-degree felony.

Revenge ("I'll post old pics") harassment: Finn's exploits are driving you crazy. You are to the point that you feel you need to strike back. You decide those text pictures that were sent when the relationship was new, exciting, and relatively healthy would be perfect ammunition. You fire up the cell phone or laptop and go to town, posting on every site you can think of. Over and above the obvious lapse in good judgment, legal implications could come. The most obvious is harassment or stalking.

As we discussed in the Chapter 5 (*The Digital Age*), this may fall under several statutes, such as general harassment as well the ones covering "cyber-bullying." Look ahead at that chapter for details. The simple and best option is don't resort to this. You can be made to look like the aggressor, so don't fall for it.

Even the secret ones: Same situation as above, but you stumble across those "secret" photos you have from that night that Finn passed out drunk and naked in your bedroom. Instead of posting, you simply send a couple out to anyone that you think might know Finn, maybe even some that don't.

Now you've upped the stakes by possibly committing the offense of improper photography, a state jail felony, as well as the harassment/cyber-bullying described above.

Finn's taking it out on the pets: Now for the last straw, neighbors see Finn abduct the stray cat you feed on the porch and it is found later on your doorstep, suffocated in a plastic bag. Finn has committed the Class A misdemeanor of cruelty to animals by torturing and ultimately killing the stray cat.

Finn cries wolf: Deep down, you always knew Finn was teetering on the brink, feeling threatened or frightened even when the situation is rather mundane and innocuous. Nonetheless, Sean had at one time went through a stage thinking someone was trying to break into the apartment. Finn quickly became well-known to the cops and they finally got tired of her continual calls for help. Finally, the 911 operator told her not to call unless there is actually an emergency. Finn's response was a terse insult. When the cops arrived this time, they actually arrested someone, Finn. Silent or abusive calls to 9-1-1 service are a Class B misdemeanor.

SEXUAL ASSAULT = RAPE

Some advocacy groups lump "date rape" and "acquaintance rape" together, taking the position that any sex act coupled with pressure is a form of rape. I certainly am not condoning the social pressures discussed earlier, but legally speaking, this is not the case. It is important to understand the definitions so you are fully informed.

A person commits the offense of sexual assault (rape), if the person intentionally or knowingly causes the penetration of:

- The anus or sexual organ of another person.
- The mouth of another person by the sexual organ of the actor, without that person's consent.
- A third person causes the sexual organ of another person to contact or penetrate the mouth, anus, or sexual organ without that person's consent.

Although sexual assault is understood as a crime of violence, it becomes "aggravated" under certain conditions, including if the perpetrator causes bodily injury, attempts to kill the victim or another person, uses or shows a deadly weapon, or administers a date rape drug to the victim.

Consent is the key to whether sex is actually a sexual assault. Sex is without the consent of the other person if:

- Someone compels another person to submit or participate by using or threats of violence.
- The "victim" has not consented and is unconscious or physically unable to resist or is unaware that the sexual assault is occurring.
- Someone who knows that as a result of mental disease or defect the other person is at the time of the sexual assault incapable of appraising the nature of the act or of resisting it.
- Coerced by a public servant, clergy member, or mental-health service provider by exploiting the person's emotional dependency.
- By intentionally administering any substance (See *Date Rape Drugs* section below for more information) without the other

person's knowledge to impair the victim's power to appraise or control her own conduct.

No means no: As I have detailed in an earlier chapter on this subject, the obvious cannot be said enough: No means NO. That being said, be unequivocal when it comes to a sexual situation that you do not want to happen. Assert yourself no matter what.

What to do ...

- If you've been sexually assaulted, take steps right away:
- Get away from the attacker to a safe place as fast as you can.
- Call a friend or family member you trust or a crisis center or hotline to talk with a counselor. One national hotline is the National Domestic Violence Hotline 800-799-SAFE or TDD 800-787-3224.
- Get counseling from a trusted professional. Feelings of shame, guilt, fear and shock are normal and need to be addressed.
- Do not wash, comb or clean any part of your body or change clothes, if possible, so the hospital staff can collect evidence.
- Do not touch or change anything at the scene of the assault.
- Go immediately to your nearest hospital emergency room. You need to be examined, treated for any injuries and screened for possible sexually transmitted diseases or pregnancy. The hospital should collect evidence using a rape kit for fibers, hairs, saliva, semen, or clothing that the attacker may have left behind. If they do not, tell them to.
- You or the hospital staff can call the police from the emergency room to file a report.

A friend has been sexually assaulted: First off, listen to what she is saying, believe her and offer comfort. Then encourage her to take the steps detailed above and go with her through the process. Reinforce the message that she is not at fault and that it is natural to feel angry and ashamed, but it is also important to go forward and disclose all details asked of them.

SEX CRIMES AND SEX OFFENDER REGISTRATION

The most punitive and long-reaching conviction that carries the biggest and worst set of baggage is a conviction or an adjudication of a sex crime. That's right, commit any crime that is a "reportable conviction or adjudication" and you will have to register as a "sex offender." Our society has placed a great emphasis on keeping close watch on sex offenders, with probably very good reason. Every state requires sex offender registration of some form or fashion. The Texas Sex Offender Registration Law requires registration for crimes that occurred all the way back to 1970.

What is a sex crime? In Texas, it's indecency with a child (by sexual contact); sexual assault; aggravated sexual assault; aggravated kidnapping with intent to sexually abuse; burglary with intent to commit sexual assault; indecency with a child (by exposure) with a prior reportable sex offense conviction; attempt/conspiracy/solicitation or commission of unlawful restraint/kidnapping/aggravated kidnapping of a child with a prior reportable sex offense conviction. All of these are also considered "sexually violent offenses." Other reportable sex crimes are prohibited sexual conduct; compelling prostitution; sexual performance by a child; possession or promotion of child pornography; attempted sexual assault; and a second conviction for indecent exposure.

College and university notification: Sex offenders working or attending college must register with campus security (or the local police) within seven days of starting class or work. If the person leaves the school, he must notify the authorities within seven days.

How long does a sex offender have to register?

Lifetime registration: A "sexually violent" crime requires annual registration for life.

Joe's "frisky" performance with his girlfriend in the park,

where the school kids get a good peak of their sexual talents, not to mention their privates, doesn't seem like a serious case, but be careful. Let's say Joe simply pleads guilty and pays a small fine. The real problem is that Joe fails to understand what exactly he pled guilty to. It is not out of the realm of possibility that if charged and convicted of indecency with a child, a conviction or deferred adjudication will force both to register as sex offenders. Usually most people in Joe's situation will be charged with indecent exposure, which does not require registration. But hold on a minute. This, too, can carry some lingering effects, because if Joe or his girlfriend are convicted again for indecent exposure, sex offender registration becomes a reality

Limited term registration: For all other "reportable convictions" that are not "sexually violent" offenses, registration is for 10 years after being discharged from prison or probation supervision. Joe and the guys in New Orleans for Mardi Gras, where they encounter the time-honored tradition of "bead baiting." For those who are uninitiated, some of the ladies who attend Mardi Gras will expose certain parts of their body for the really good beads. Generally speaking, the authorities turn their heads unless it gets really out of hand. Joe decides that he'll get into the action and shows off his "trouser trout" in exchange for some beads. (By the way, the New Orleans cops consider this "getting out of hand.") As he unzips and whips it out, the cops crack him in the head with their flashlight and drag him off to jail for indecent exposure. Because of his earlier problem in the park with his girlfriend and his cavalier attitude in pleading guilty, this is his second offense. If convicted, he becomes a registered sex offender. (See *Girls Gone Wild* section of Chapter 5 for more of Joe's exploits in this area).

It's a crime not to register: Failure to register as a sex offender is a state jail or third-degree felony, depending on the offense. There are quite a lot of technical requirements under the registration statute and all must be strictly followed, otherwise a registrant may be prosecuted for a completely separate crime.

What else do convicted sex offenders have to do? Over and above the threat of a long prison term, there's the likelihood of having personal information published and being listed in a public database.

Certain things may come along with probation, such being required to submit a blood sample or other specimen for a DNA database and to submit to treatment, specialized supervision or rehabilitation.

If the victim of the sex crime was a child, the judge will establish a "child safety zone" by ordering the sex offender to stay more than 1,000 feet from places children gather, such as schools and playgrounds. He will also be forbidden from participating in any program that includes children.

The term of probation may even be extended by the court if for 10 more years if the judge determines that the probationer has not sufficiently demonstrated a commitment to avoid future criminal behavior and that the release of the defendant from supervision would endanger the public.

Creative judges have been known to require offenders to post a sign on their front door alerting the community that they are a sex offender or to personally notify their neighbors that they are a sex offender.

REPRODUCTIVE RIGHTS, ABORTION, ADOPTION AND PATERNITY

Birth control: According to some estimates, 85 percent of women who use no contraceptive become pregnant each year. The only guarantee against pregnancy is not having intercourse. There are other contraceptive methods that greatly reduce the risk of pregnancy, including condoms, diaphragms, birth control pills, Depo-Provera injections, IUDs (intrauterine devices), cervical caps and fertility awareness methods. Women should ask their doctor during their annual gynecological exam for advice.

Pro-life or pro-choice: Everyone seems to have definitive feelings on this particular subject. Politicians, civil rights groups and religious organizations, each with their own agenda, actively advocate their position on the subject. Although legal, many people in our society refuse to accept this and diligently work to change the status of the law, some becoming religious zealots and violent extremists, orchestrating a campaign of intimidation and terror aimed at women seeking abortions and the health professionals who work at family planning clinics. Ironically, some even take the position that the termination of a fetus' viability is so heinous it justifies the murder of those participating in this legal activity. Some even take the position that victims of rape or incest should be forced to bear the child.

Whatever your opinion, I respect it and this section is not intended to try to persuade you either way. I will try to give an objective overview, keeping in mind that the law is the primary focus and what is or is not legally available to women.

Restrictions and limitations on abortion in Texas.

When is it an option? As of October 29, 2013, abortion is legal before the 20th week of gestation (22 weeks if calculated from the last monthly period), however there are restrictions. An abortion during third trimester of viable child is permissible only if necessary to prevent death or if there is substantial risk of serious impairment to the woman's physical or mental health, or if the fetus has severe and irreversible abnormality.

Where is it available? If seeking abortion-inducing medications (such as RU-486), women must make four visits to a licensed physician. Surgical abortions must be performed in a licensed surgical facility that meets Board of Health standards and reports to Department of Health.

What is required?

Minimum visits: As of October 1, 2011, women seeking an abortion must have at least two visits to the abortion facility: the first for an ultrasound, the second for the procedure.

24-hour ultrasound: In the summer of 2011, the Texas Legislature passed a bill that requires women to have an ultrasound at least 24 hours before she has an abortion, be shown the image, and have the image described to her. Many women's rights advocates and medical professionals argue that this is not medically necessary, nor is there any medical reason for requiring women to come 24 hours in advance. Traditionally, ultrasounds have been a standard part of reputable medical providers who perform abortion services and are usually performed on every patient before any type of procedure is done.

"Women's Right to Know Act": The Texas Legislature also passed the "Women's Right To Know Act," which requires physicians to give women seeking abortions state-mandated information about medical risks, adoption alternatives and developmental stages of the fetus. This information must be provided 24 hours in advance of the abortion procedure during the first visit when the woman receives her required ultrasound.

Medication abortion: An early, non-surgical abortion done with pills will require up to four visits with the same doctor. First, 24 hours in advance for a sonogram. Then for the first and second doses of the drug. Follow-up within 14 days is also required.

Emergency contraception: Formerly known as the "morning-after pill," this is a special dose of commonly prescribed birth control pills that can help to prevent pregnancy when taken within three days of a birth-control accident or unprotected sex. It may work by preventing ovulation, fertilization, or implantation but does not cause an abortion. This is also commonly called "medication abortion." Emergency contraception does not prevent HIV or other sexually transmitted infections. Recent legal rulings have affected the access to these alternatives, but the fight by both sides on this issue continues.

Teenagers: Texas requires that one parent must be informed at least 48 hours before the abortion performed if the person is under eighteen. But the teen does not need to obtain permission. There is an alternative, which involves applying to a judge to waive this requirement. Planned Parenthood is a good resource for the latest information.

Have a voice — be heard, get involved: If you agree with these restrictions or advocate for further restrictions, I encourage you to let your representatives know that. If you feel that these restrictions impair, restrict or otherwise negatively impact your rights or the rights of women generally, let them know. If you feel that the government should not be legislating any particular religious, moral or ethical beliefs, then let them know that also. Lastly, this is an issue that is uniquely a "woman's issue," so use your right to vote to let your legislators know what your opinion is by electing those who share your opinion or fight for those issues that your agree with.

More info: The "Women's Right to Know" information is available on the Texas Department of State Health Services website or can be picked up at any Planned Parenthood clinic. The Texas Department of State Health Services is also responsible for complaints. You can write Director, Health Facility Licensing and Compliance Division, Texas Department of State Health Services, 1100 West 49th Street, Austin, TX 78756 or call 1-888-973-0022. Complainants must provide their name.

Pro-life alternatives: There are nearly 3,000 Crisis Pregnancy Centers throughout the U.S. staffed by volunteers who provide pregnancy tests and counseling, but also offer a full range of services. These facilities and programs offer and arrange pre- and post-natal medical care, as well as help women obtain housing, maternity and baby clothes, baby equipment, legal assistance and financial support. They focus on offering alternatives to abortion, even advice concerning single-parenting issues, as well as real and tangible assistance, helping thousands of women to choose other alternatives, rather than choosing to undergo an abortion.

Adoption: Adoption is another alternative option. An adoption is the legal transfer of parental rights from the natural or birth parents to the adoptive parents. The adoptive parents become legally responsible for the child and obtain all legal parental rights with regard to the child. A new birth certificate is even issued for the child, reflecting the adoptive parents' names as the child's mother and father at the time of birth. The original is retained, but sealed and accessible only by court order. An adoption in Texas may be open, closed, anonymous, private or through an agency, or some combination. Some adoptions even take place within a family, known also as a relative adoption (i.e. stepparent, grandparent, aunt, uncle etc.) and it is even possible for an adult to be adopted by another, older adult, but only with consent, which is also required for adopting a child over the age of 12.

Any adult in Texas may file a petition to adopt a child, usually married couples, although single, separated, and divorced people have the right to adopt in Texas as well. There are no legal standards for adoption as to age, housing situation, social background, or income level and Texas law forbids discrimination in adoption because of race or ethnicity.

The consent of the birth mother may not be obtained until 48 hours after the child is born, witnessed by two people and verified by a notary. Once the birth mother has signed the relinquishment form, it cannot be revoked for 60 days. During this 60-day period, a judge decides whether to accept the consent form and terminate parental rights. Once the court enters a final adoption order, the new birth certificate is issued and the legal rights and responsibilities of parenting go into effect and may not be challenged by the birth parents or other parties.

It is a third-degree felony to offer to buy or sell a baby in Texas, which means that the adoptive parents may not pay a parent or a third person for the right to adopt a child, but are allowed to pay reasonable expenses in connection with the adoption.

Adoption records: Adoptive parents, legal guardians of adopted adults and adopted adults may obtain non-identifying information of the adoption. Adopted adults 18 or older, birth parents, and birth siblings 21 or older can obtain identifying information of their biological parents through a registry provided through the agency or the Texas Department of Health-Bureau of Vital Statistics. An adoptee must petition the court in which the adoption was finalized to obtain the sealed original birth certificate.

Who's the father? Establishing paternity: When a child is born, the mother's husband is presumed to be the father. This includes "common-law" marriages at the time and a marriage within 300 days of birth. Why 300 days? This is to take account of situations where the birth-mother was married at the time of conception, but the marriage was ended by divorce, annulment, or death during the pregnancy, thus making the ex-husband or deceased husband the presumed father. If someone other than the ex-husband is the biological father, the husband may give up his parental rights by completing the denial of paternity section on an acknowledgment of paternity document.

If the mother is not married at the time of the birth or within 300 days of the birth, by law there is no presumed father and any man claiming to be the father, with the mother's consent, may establish paternity by executing an acknowledgment of paternity form either at birth or anytime thereafter.

If a man believes he is the father of the child, but the mother disagrees or the husband does not agree to release his paternity rights, a notice of intent to claim paternity may be filed by the man claiming to be the father.

Why should I establish paternity for my child? Most people are of the opinion that all kids should at least know who their biological father is, no matter who raises them, but more important, the child may be entitled to government benefits such as Social Security, veterans benefits, health care, insurance, etc., through the father. Once paternity is acknowledged or established, the child can receive all the benefits he is entitled. Without it, the child cannot even receive court-ordered child support payments. Knowing the biological father will also provide helpful and sometimes vital information for future medical treatment. This information can only be gained from knowing who the father is and therefore, his family medical history for future medical treatment of the child.

Father's rights: Once the father is established, he becomes a natural guardian of the minor child and has the right to take legal action on behalf of the child in certain circumstances. A paternity case is a lawsuit to determine the natural and legal father of a minor child and to confer to him the rights and duties of a parent. Once the father has been determined to be the biological father, he obtains certain rights, such as visitation, but also the obligations for financial support. The mother of the child must also consult and discuss with the father various child-rearing subjects, such as religion, education, medical care and vacations. An unmarried biological father even has the right to obtain custody of the minor child, if appropriate and have a say in how the child is raised and cared for, the same rights as a married father.

Child support: Any parent not having custody of a child is at least responsible to financially assist in supporting that child. Generally speaking, the amount of child support owed is according to a formula, ranging from 20 percent of the payer's resources for one child to at least 40 percent for six or more children.

The non-custodial parent is also required to maintain the children on their employment health insurance policy, if possible, or alternatively pay the amount necessary to maintain insurance coverage to the extent coverage is available and affordable.

Child support orders and obligations generally continue until the child reaches age 18 or until the child graduates from high school. In the event a child is disabled, child support may continue indefinitely. All orders relating to the custody and support of children may be modified by the court or by agreement between the parties, but remember that informal agreements are not legally binding. If such an agreement is reached, contact an attorney to have the court enter an order pursuant to the agreement; otherwise, someone may be in violation of the court's orders.

Child support payments are enforceable and failure to pay

child support can result in garnishment of wages, tax refunds and even imprisonment. Even if visitation is not being allowed by the custodial parent, child support payments must continue and cannot be withheld. Visitation and child support payments are separate issues.

The Texas Attorney General is the official child support enforcement agency for the state of Texas, and provides services for parents seeking support for their children. Contact the Texas attorney general for more information at 800-252-8014.

CHAPTER 5
THE DIGITAL AGE

CELLS PHONES AND SOCIAL MEDIA

THIS SUBJECT IS SO UBIQUITOUS to our lives these days that it could be a book all on its own, but I'll try to keep it short. I am not even going to touch upon the debate regarding potential negative impacts on mental health, physical health, social skills, or other psychological and sociological aspects that electronics may affect.

First, always remember that if it's online it's probably forever. That means that anyone may be able to look back in time to see what you were doing way back when. This has become a gold mine for those who want to investigate people, their motives and backgrounds. It is quite popular for companies, prospective employers and prosecutors to take a quick peek into what may be left behind in your digital footprints to see if you are the person that they see before them. Those photos shot-gunning a beer will be very interesting to a prosecutor, should you be arrested for DWI or public intoxication, for instance. Such things can also be used to determine where and when someone may have been somewhere, especially when they have suggested that they were somewhere else.

Keep your profiles clean. Request photos you don't like to be taken down and don't post anything that you don't want to be seen. Don't text anything that you don't mean or that can be misinterpreted. Don't send an email or post a hateful or threatening rant in the heat of the moment.

Things like that can be taken out of context and used to make you look like something you are not.

TOOL FOR PERSONAL PROTECTION

Many may argue that a firearm is the best tool to protect yourself, however your cell phone is probably the best, safest and most accessible tool you have. Its camera and recording capabilities can be used on a daily basis to protect yourself. Video and audio continues to find new and valuable uses as evidence. It can be supportive should you be accused of doing something or even help verify a situation where you are the victim. Examples of ways it can be used are:

Documenting threatening behavior.

- Documenting damages (or lack thereof) to property.
- Photographing receipts of payment or saving documents like leases or agreements.
- Location apps that allow people to find where you may be located.
- Saving emergency contacts in your favorite contacts.
- Saving emergency medical information where it can be found easily.

Let's say our new friend Joe accidentally scrapes the side of a parked car. He stops, but cannot locate the owner. He leaves a note on the windshield with his name, driver's license number, phone number, insurance policy information and the time of the accident. He puts the note under the windshield and then takes several photos of the damage. The next day he gets a call from the police suggesting he had been identified as the driver of a vehicle that left the scene of an accident. Additionally, his insurance company called to inform him that a claim for approximately $10,000 in repairs had been filed. Luckily, he provided the police and the insurance company the photos. No criminal charges were filed and the insurance fraud was discovered, as well as the false report. Joe saved himself from a lot of problems by taking two minutes to document the incident.

What and where can you record? Generally speaking, anyone in a public place can take a picture of anything they want, even other people. If you can see it, you can shoot it. Even private property that is open to the public is fair game. However, if you're asked not to while on private property or there are signs posted to that effect, you're obliged to obey. Concerts and movie theaters are good examples where recording oftentimes leads to piracy and therefore is restricted as a condition of your admission. Taking pictures of other people in public is OK, but not if they are trying to be private. I doubt it would be OK to take pictures of someone entering his PIN code at the store, but taking pictures of people loading their groceries, while creepy, is generally OK. Areas where people expect privacy, like public bathrooms, are also off-limits.

Security is often a word used to justify the restriction of photographing something, a place or event, but is usually just an excuse from someone who just doesn't like the idea, probably because they are simply following orders or doing something they shouldn't be doing. Whatever the real reason, it is rarely a valid reason. As long as you are not obstructing a police officer or other emergency personnel, accident scenes, crime scenes and police activities are subject to recording. While all of this may be considered legal, you may find yourself confronted. Always be polite and non-confrontational. Usually these are high-stress situations and you don't want to contribute to the chaos. Ask yourself if what you are recording is important enough to stand your ground and act accordingly. You do not have to identify yourself (except in some circumstances if asked by a police officer), nor can anyone legally make you stop or forcibly take the camera/phone away from you. If someone does forcibly take your camera/phone or physically assaults you, consider taking action. Call the police and report it or if it is an employee of a company, go above his head and report the behavior to his superiors. If it's the police acting up, file a report with the department, contact the media or even post it online for everyone to see.

Sexting, texting and digital images: The past couple of decades have presented us humans many new ways to share our thoughts, opinions, as well as communicate, which can include some of our needs to do so in sexually explicit ways. Sexting has evolved from simple dirty talk to sending nude photos or videos.

In a perfect world you should be able to send a nudie to your boyfriend or girlfriend at another college without fearing it will end up as someone else's screensaver. We do not live in a perfect world and cannot control what other people do, so at the very least follow a few rules so you can reduce the chance that your sext doesn't ruin your life.

As we discussed earlier, doing so puts your personal privacy at great risk, and you give your control over to whoever may come across your photos to use for their own pleasure, amusement or exploitation.

Just think about explaining to Mom and Dad why you're the new YouTube sensation or why your new boss has a picture of your junk sent to her by a co-worker. Remember that those nudie pics will remain with her even after the relationship ends. Situations may arise where they end up being passed around or even posted for public consumption if the relationship suffers an acrimonious end. Revenge is a common response to rejection or betrayal, so remember that when you're getting ready to hit send.

It seems that people just simply like to send dirty pictures, however my advice is don't do it. But if you choose to do so, consider a few hints that may help protect your privacy for all eternity, if possible:

- Keep your face or any distinguishing marks or tattoos out of the picture.
- Know what is in the background. Family photos, or other items that may help identify you sort of defeats your goal anonymity.
- Avoid sending by email or text. Use an app, like Snapchat that

allows you to destroy the image after a view or short viewing time limit.
- Send a little warning message before it goes live to someone. This may avoid someone you don't want to see it from an accidental view.
- Don't do it just because someone pressures you in to it. If they are pressuring you, then they may have some other reason for asking.
- Double and triple check who your recipients are. A mistaken text to "Dad" or "Mom," "send all" or some lingering text thread exchange might be a rather embarrassing mistake.
- Make sure you trust the person who you send to. Do not send those nudies to some random you just met at a party or matched with on Tinder. Before sending, you better be 100 percent sure that the boyfriend/girlfriend knows this is for his/her eyes only. Otherwise, you may become the home screen wallpaper for the frat.
- You better make sure you know, for sure, the age of the recipient. Just because she said she was a certain age is no defense to criminal prosecution (See below).

Adults involved with sexting with minors can be prosecuted if the contents of the electronic communications contain images of a minor. Charges vary, but could be possessing or distributing child pornography, promoting sexual performance by a minor and soliciting a minor.

Sexting between teens in Texas can also be trouble. It is illegal to electronically transmit sexual depictions of children, even for one minor to electronically send an image of someone younger than 18 to another minor; this includes images of the sender, recipient, or another underage person. There is a defense to prosecution for a minor when the images are solely of the sender or recipient, if they were sent within a dating relationship, and if both parties are not more than two years apart in age (including if one party is 18 or older).

Secret recordings: Taking pictures of other people is not always OK. Making your own "sex tape" is perfectly legal. It may be a romantic or naughty indulgence between two consenting adults, but remember that they too can get out into the digital world and remain long after the relationship has ended.

Secretly recording your exploits, however, is illegal.

Joe is walking to class as he passes by his neighbor's window. He is standing on the sidewalk, but the shades are open and he can see down the hallway and thought the open door into the bedroom, where his neighbor is toweling off after a shower. He knows the neighbor, so as a prank, he pulls out his phone, shoots it and posts to Vine and YouTube. BANG, Joe has committed a felony.

Snapping a few of your neighbor undressing, even though you are on the sidewalk and can see through the drapes, again, is not OK. In fact, it is a state jail felony to photograph, videotape, record, broadcast, or transmit a visual image of another without the other person's consent if there's intent to arouse or gratify the sexual desire of any person. This is usually the "peeping tom" situation, but also applies to that secretly recorded sex tape your friend suggested. It also involves bathrooms and dressing rooms, adding an optional element that it was done so "with the intent to invade the privacy of the other person." It's also a crime to send, post, copy, record or otherwise transmit any image that the person knows was made in this manner.

Joe's girlfriend is over spending the night. He surreptitiously records their sexual encounter. BANG, (no pun intended), he has committed a felony.

Joe also thinks it might be funny to secretly film his roommate taking a shower and going through his morning routine before classes. While the tape captures no particularly revealing body parts of the roommate, it does document some of his roommate's more embarrassing hygiene rituals. Joe posts another Vine and BANG, again commits a felony. Although a prank, it was clearly meant to "invade the privacy" of his roommate.

Just in case you were wondering, a sign posted in a bathroom or dressing room saying you're being photographed or recorded does not mean you've consented and does not make it OK.

ELECTRONIC HARRASSMENT

Electronic or digital harassment is just like any other, and if you persistently text, email or otherwise contact someone through electronic means and if the content is threatening or is perceived as such, you could possibly face criminal charges.

Cyber-bullying: This is has become more prevalent and has been blamed on suicide and other tragic results. Texas has enacted a fairly general statute intended to address cyber-bullying and online harassment. Although not specifically addressed as such, it more accurately encompasses online harassment through impersonation. Commonly referred to as "cyberstalking," many of these situations involve former lovers, but can also include impersonating strangers, neighbors and classmates.

It is a felony to use the name or persona of another person to create a web page or post on a social networking site if the action is taken to harm, threaten, defraud or intimidate the other person.

Defamation, libel and slander: These related terms are often confused, however each involves false statements. What form they're in determines which category they fall under.

- Defamation: This is the catch-all term for libelous and or slanderous statements.
- Libel: Written defamation. This includes the modern evolutionary forms such as content found on websites, comments, blog posts, bulletin board posts.
- Slander: Spoken word defamation. This includes podcasts, video and audio files or even transcriptions of the video and audio.

Obviously the Internet has become an ever-increasingly crowded battlefield for people and companies seeking to protect themselves from unwarranted postings. On one side of the debate is free speech. On the other is the protection of people and commercial enterprises from the proliferation of false information.

Successfully attacking a statement, in any form requires:

- Proof that the statement is in fact false. Opinions are typically not actionable.
- Proof that the false statement harms your reputation and causes some harm.
- The false statement must be made without due diligence or research regarding its truthfulness. Knowledge of the statement's falsity is of great relevance, as well.
- If the statement is related to celebrity, public figure or official, malice must also be present (i.e. an intent to harm or reckless disregard of the truth).

Generally speaking, satirical speech and writing is excluded, and while it may be difficult to successfully bring a lawsuit, protecting a person's or business's reputation is important. Given the rise in situations that may cause alarm to those who are the targets of such attacks, companies and organizations that assist in clearing false information have become more prevalent.

There have even been successful lawsuits against individuals who post to comment boards and social network sites anonymously. Digital evidence led to the identification of the posters, which in turn identified the sources of the defamation. The lesson: You should post only facts that you know, otherwise be sure you make it clear that it is your opinion and not a statement of fact, otherwise your ranting may come back to bite you in the wallet.

COMPUTERS AND HACKING

Texas computer crimes: Our old friend Joe is surfing the Internet one afternoon while sitting around the dorm room. Schmedley, the geek from down the hall, wanders by and they begin to talk computers. The subject of "hacking" comes up and Schmedley jumps on Joe's computer and quickly hacks into the university's mainframe and looks around. BANG, they have committed the offense of breach of computer security.

Texas law makes it a crime to knowingly access another person's computer, computer network, or computer system without the "effective consent of the owner." Originally, it was required that the person "breach" a computer security system in order to commit the offense. This requirement has since been removed by the legislature. "Effective consent" basically means permission to access the internal workings, files, programs, etc. of a computer or a network. Such access is always without "effective consent" if it is without the knowledge of the owner of the computer or network. The key to this offense is the broad definition of the term access, which not only includes altering data or computer software in the computer, but also making use of the computer, even if there is absolutely no damage or alterations to the information, files, data or programs. Merely getting in and snooping around constitutes a crime.

Authorized use for an unauthorized purpose is also a crime.

Joe has recently secured gainful employment in the school's data entry department, entering information and inventory information. One afternoon, he decides to browse student files and grades. BANG, Joe has accessed files and information that he does not have authorization or "effective consent" to look at, much less alter.

While working for the university, Joe has been given access to passwords to the university's computer network, which he quickly gives to Schmedley, the geek down the hall. BANG, he has again committed an offense by his unauthorized distribution of this type of information, which includes identifying codes, PIN numbers, debit card numbers, bank account numbers and any other "confidential information about a computer security system."

Joe has committed a Class B misdemeanor, but his crime may be elevated to a Class A misdemeanor if there was any intent to obtain a benefit or defraud or harm another person. If the value or benefit to Joe or the loss suffered by the university exceeds $1,500, it's a state jail felony; over $20,000 and it's a third degree felony.

This is the primary statute used in state prosecutions, but other more specific protections exist for computers and data, including federal laws protecting federal government computers and those used in interstate commerce.

The feds and computers: The federal law is similar to the laws in Texas, but goes into a little more detail dealing with specific types of computers. The basic federal computer crimes specifically deal with unauthorized use of computers and the alteration or destruction of the records and data they contain. The severity of the offense depends on whether the computer hacked is a "federal interest computer" or contains national security, financial or credit information, or uses more than two computers in more than one state, which is almost always the case.

Criminal penalties range from a fine of up to $100,000 and up to one year in prison up to 20 years in a federal prison.

As you can see, Texas and federal law are relatively parallel and may be prosecuted by either state or federal prosecutors. No matter who investigates or prosecutes, there are certain instances that may be prosecuted in both state and federal courts for the same activity, notwithstanding traditional notions of double jeopardy.

Solicitation of a minor: So you have stumbled into a chat room and on the other end is someone who claims to be 14 years old and you begin to chat. The chat turns sexual and some really provocative suggestions are made. Be careful, even if you are just joking around, this can be taken very seriously. This has become a popular undercover operation and may very well be a sting. You may very well be chatting with a law enforcement agent who is setting you up for a fall, even if you're not serious about what you are saying.

The scariest part of this type of offense is that it is not a defense that the person on the other end of the chat is not actually a minor, but only that the person accused believes that the person is a minor (under 17) and makes the wrong suggestion or comment. Joking around can get you into trouble, even if you didn't mean to, so be careful of what you're saying and to whom it is being said.

Porn and the Internet: You are surfing the 'net and stumble upon images of some homemade photos of what appear to be the local high school cheerleading squad, posing in some explicit and compromising positions. As a prank, you send them to everyone in your address book and the images are saved on your hard drive. This may very well be considered "child pornography." Does that mean that the FBI is watching or about to bust through the door? Probably not, but as Internet privacy issues continue to be contested and revelations about the NSA are exposed, only your imagination can fathom the future developments of the Internet and related technologies.

While adult pornography on the Internet is subject to First Amendment protections, child pornography holds no such rights, and all state laws deem the trafficking of child porn images a felony. Possession of child pornography, on the other hand, is in many states classified as a misdemeanor. What is or is not "child pornography" will continue to be subject to legal scrutiny, judicial review and the subject of criminal investigations and subsequent prosecutions. What makes this particular area of law so scary is that the viewer or possessor of these images does not have to "know" that the people depicted are actually children, but merely appear to be minors. If it sounds like it's difficult to determine exactly what is or is not against the law, that's because it is, for the most part. Many scenarios have already arisen and many more will follow.

Internet service providers are not required by law to police their networks, with the result being that many pornography web sites operate with impunity until complaints are lodged with local law enforcement or the Department of Justice.

What should you do to protect yourself? If you do stumble upon these types of images or are suspicious, your best bet is to make sure you don't download them or send them to others. To the best of your computer skills, destroy those images and stay away from the sites that promote such images.

It is safe to assume that your communications over the Internet are not necessarily confidential and someone may very well be watching, intercepting, or keeping a record of your communications. Jokes, pranks, and fantasy can be interpreted in many different ways, so use some restraint when communicating over the Internet to ensure that such words are not taken out of context or interpreted to your detriment.

CHAPTER 6
ADULT VS. 21

You have made it out of high school and have embarked on the pursuit of a college education. Good for you, and keep at it. This also means that for the vast majority of those who are reading this, you have also just moved to school and out from under the loving but watchful eye of your parental unit(s). One other assumption is that you are probably at least 17 or 18 years old. Now, I certainly understand that you see yourself as an adult and full well can act as such. Turning 18 means that you have become saddled with the full responsibilities and liabilities heaped upon all of us, but without the fun. It ain't fair, but that's the way it is.

17 AND 18

Once you turn 18, you are an adult and are expected to act accordingly. According to the criminal laws in Texas, you are an adult upon turning 17 and you can be prosecuted as an adult. The old myth that juvenile criminal records are sealed or destroyed is no longer true. It is true criminal convictions cannot be used to enhance future adult punishments, however it can be taken into consideration when a judge or jury is determining an appropriate sentence. If you have not turned 18, you may still have some form of curfew, so check with the authorities so you know exactly what it is.

VOTING

This is most important right that vests once you are 18. Take this new right to heart and vote every opportunity you can. Sadly, 18- to 24-year-olds vote less than any other group. So if all these laws targeted at you don't motivate you to educate yourself and prompt you to vote for those who will represent your interest, you will probably continue to see more and more restrictions on your freedoms.

If you attend college away from home and are registered to vote at your parents' address, you have several voting options. You may register to vote at your new college residence or keep your voter registration at your parents' address. You decide where you reside for voting purposes, but you cannot register in both locations. If you keep your voter registration at your parents' address and will not be home during the early voting period or on Election Day, you can request that a ballot by mail be sent to you at your college address.

I suggest that you register to vote in the town in which you are going to school. It is where you spend the most time and where you are most affected by the local government. It's your home. Why shouldn't it reflect the will of the people who live there? Most colleges have political clubs and societies that may interest you. Being registered to vote will be an important part of the participation. Who knows? You may even meet a member of the opposite sex who has the same political views as you or maybe just someone with whom you can argue and then go have a beer. Voting impacts almost every aspect of our lives, so get out there and vote. An old college professor of mine always preached, "If you don't vote, you don't have the right to bitch about what your government is doing."

Suffrage, although it sounds bad, is actually a very good thing. It is the right to vote and began way before we embraced the concept in forming the United States. Centuries ago, in the Greek city-states, all freemen were expected to take part in the government of their city, although the freeman population was a minority of the population. There were no "career politicians," as they served as representatives for short terms on a rotating/lottery-style basis. Ancient Rome incorporated certain voting rights in its government by allowing the common citizens, called plebs, the right to elect tribunes, which would represent them to address unfair or oppressive treatment by the government. Even before Columbus arrived, the Native American Iroquois nation embraced its own style of democracy, which employed a citizen-run government and even included women tribe members.

The U.S. Constitution originally allowed each state to determine its voter qualifications; but the states' inabilities to incorporate constitutionally valid qualifications resulted in a national call for change. Amendments to the U.S. Constitution were necessary to prohibit states from denying the right to vote based on race or sex or charging a poll tax in national elections. Literacy tests were also used to keep certain "undesirable" persons from voting, usually the black populations of the southern states. The Civil Rights Act of 1965 put a stop to that by banning such restrictions in any state that had less than 50 percent of the population registered to vote.

In 1970 the U.S. Supreme Court ruled that 18-year-olds had the right to vote in all federal elections (the age limit in most states was 21). The 26th Amendment to the Constitution made this a right in all elections in 1971.

JURY DUTY

Another right you are now vested with is the right to serve on a jury, commonly referred to as jury duty. You owe it to your country, your local government, your fellow citizens, and to yourself to appear for jury service. Many people see jury service as a huge pain in the ass, taking them away from their daily lives and responsibilities. But you should see it for what it truly is: the closest and most direct impact you can have on the function of our government.

The U.S. and Texas constitutions guarantee a right to trial by jury for anyone accused of a crime, regardless of race, religion, gender, national origin or economic status. So important, that it was even included in the Texas Declaration of Independence. Any time the facts of a civil or criminal case are in dispute, the parties have a right to have their case heard by a jury of fair and impartial citizens who will make decisions without bias or prejudice.

The concept of a jury trial is hardly new, dating to medieval England, but it is not a concept that has been adopted by many societies. The vast majority of countries consider it insane that we put the power to decide what is against the law, who committed a crime, and many other important decisions in the hands of citizens. In the United States the power lies in the people, not the government, The jury system is just one more way the citizens are vested with the power to make sure that the government is doing what the people feel is best for the country and not the other way around.

Obviously, to have a jury trial, you've got to have a jury; and to have a jury, citizens from all walks of life must be called upon to participate. That's where you come into the picture. Because you have received a jury summons, you are now placed in a position of power most people in the world will never experience. You have the opportunity to see the justice system up close. If selected to serve on a jury, you will participate in one of this country's most fundamental processes.

Qualifications to be a juror:

- At least 18, a U.S. citizen, and a resident of the county in which you are called to serve.
- Qualified under the constitution and laws to vote in the county in which one is to serve as a juror. (you do not have to be a registered voter to serve).
- Of sound mind and good moral character.
- Able to read, write, and speak English.

- Has not served as a juror for six days in the preceding six months in a district court or six days in the preceding three months in a county court.
- Has not been convicted of a theft or any felony.
- Is not under indictment or other legal accusation for a theft or any felony.

Now that you have a better look at jury duty and who can be a juror, you may be wondering how you're called for jury service. If you are a registered voter, have a Texas driver's license or Texas personal identification card, your name is entered in a computer system that randomly selects prospective jurors.

Don't worry, you won't get called over and over, and you are exempted if you have served within the past 36 months.

What about my job and school? The law protects your job while you are fulfilling your jury duty. Your employer does not have to pay you, but it can't fire you for fulfilling your duty. This applies to school, as well. You may have to make up the work, but your attendance will be excused with either an excuse from the court or a phone call from the judge to the professor or department head, maybe even the dean or president. Judges usually don't like anyone who disrupts their ability to hold court. If you are attending school, you can exercise an exemption and be excused.

What to wear? Jury service is serious business, and you should dress accordingly. When you head out for jury duty, you may want to take a book, homework or other reading material to pass the time. Jury duty involves a certain amount of idle time and waiting, so come prepared to be patient. Plan to spend the day and if you're cut loose early, consider it a reward for serving your country. Some courts have dress codes, so dress appropriately. That doesn't mean a suit, but cutoffs, tank tops and flip-flops won't cut it either. Be respectful of the courts, their staff and your fellow jurors.

Juror de-selection: During jury selection, the lawyers are not deciding who they want on the jury, they are deciding who they don't want. Prospective jurors are assigned to smaller groups, may fill out questionnaires and are taken to a courtroom by a bailiff. They're briefed by the judge and may be asked questions about thier opinions about a variety of issues and subjects. There are no wrong answers; be candid if you have an opinion. Each side is given a certain number of strikes that they can use on anyone they do not want on the jury. The first six or 12 (depending on the court) people on the panel who have not been struck or excused by the judge are then "selected" for the jury.

I can't serve. As mentioned before, some people see this incredible right as a pain in the ass and lots of these same types ask me how they can get out of jury duty. As I have mentioned before, I don't think that this is the way to look at it. But since we live a in free society, they too are entitled to their opinion, even if it is exactly this type of duty that guarantees their right to that opinion. For these people, I'm going to make them read some more before I tell them the real secrets to getting out of being "selected" on a jury. Lots of times, people can't serve because they have other things planned that they can't reschedule, if that's the case, contact the district, county, or court clerk listed on the summons to try to re-schedule your service to a time that is more convenient. Most clerks have such procedures in place and are more than happy to try to accommodate your schedule in advance.

Exemptions from Service: There are some exemptions from service, which do not disqualify you, but let you out if you want:

- If you're over 70.
- People with legal custody of children under 10 when jury service would leave those children without adequate supervision (this does not apply to those who work outside the home during normal business hours or those whose children are in a daycare facility during the day).
- Students in high school or attending an institution of higher education (you must be enrolled and attending classes at the time you are summoned to appear).
- People associated with the legislative branch as an officer or an employee of the senate, house of representatives, or any

department, commission, board, office, or other agency in the legislative branch of state government.

- People who have appeared as a juror in the county during the 36 month period preceding the date he or she is to appear. (This does not apply to those who have served in a city of federal court).
- People who are primary caretakers of those unable to care for themselves (this does not apply to health care workers).
- People who have a medical condition and submit physician's documentation of such with a sworn affidavit.

There are several common misconceptions regarding exemptions that are NOT reasons for exemption:

- Being the sole owner of a business or commission sales.
- Having an employer who will not pay you for your jury service.
- Travel frequently for business.
- Having a lack of transportation.

This SUCKS, how do I get out of it? OK, those who really don't want to serve on a jury but don't qualify for an exemption will have to show up and sit through jury. I hope that this is pure hell for you and it seems like an eternity. I tell jurors all the time that a sure-fire way to get put on a jury is to sit there and say absolutely nothing, because when I go back to review my notes and jury chart, I don't have any reason to strike them. It is usually those prospective jurors who volunteer, raise their hands and are outspoken about a question or issue raised that end up getting struck by one side or the other. Jurors who categorically state that they cannot follow the law, are unable to swear an oath to follow the law or state that they are biased against one side or the other are most always excused for cause by the judge. Be forewarned, this is not some trick to try in the courtroom. Prospective jurors have been held in contempt for their antics and outspoken behavior. If the judge feels you are being obstreperous, disruptive, or disingenuous, you may be held in contempt and ordered to do something much worse than serve on a jury, like sit in a jail cell. In one instance, a judge ordered a prospective juror to attend every day of the trial and submit to the judge at the end of each week a hand-written report of the week's developments at trial. The trial lasted months.

Getting paid for jury service: Jurors receive $6 to $50 a day. Now don't get all excited, hopefully that will pay for your lunch, maybe.

The long and the short of it is that it is one more right you have, so use it. Don't let the government use or abuse it. If you do nothing else to get involved, just do this one task that makes the whole system work.

SELECTIVE SERVICE AND THE DRAFT

That's right, once you men turn 18, you're obligated to register for the draft, and some schools require it for admission. If you have a driver's license, your registration is automatic with your renewal. If you don't have a license, you can register at any U.S. Post Office. This section is mainly for the guys, since women have never been subject to forced military service and are exempted from registration. Although women are exempted from the draft, the U.S. military is certainly open to women and will gladly accept your enlistment.

Do you have to register? Probably so, with few exceptions, all male United States citizens and male aliens residing in the United States and its territories must register within 30 days of their 18th birthday. Parolees, refugees, and applicants for asylum are considered to be residents of the United States and therefore must register within 30 days of their 18th birthday. Even disabled men who are able to function in public, with or without assistance, must register The law even requires that you keep the information in your registration record up to date, notifying the Selective Service each time you move within 10 days of the relocation. This requirement is not readily enforced, but it is a requirement. This only applies to men 18 through 25. After you reach 26, there is no requirement to update your registration record.

Why do I need to comply? As stated earlier, it is the law, albeit one that is not actively prosecuted. Nonetheless, federal and many state laws require registration-age men to be registered with Selective Service to remain eligible for applying for the following benefits: job training, student financial aid, government employment, employment with the U.S. Postal Service, and U.S. citizenship for immigrants.

How to register? Besides the automatic registration linked to the driver's license, you can register in the following ways:

- At the Selective Service website, sss.gov.
- Pick up a form at the Post Office.
- If you're living or visiting overseas go to the nearest U.S. embassy or consular office where personnel will assist in registering.

You are not officially registered until your registration information is entered into the Selective Service registration file and you have been assigned a Selective Service Number.

You will then receive a registration acknowledgment card in the mail showing the information recorded in your registration file, your Selective Service Number, and a change of information form.

If you do not receive your registration acknowledgment card within 90 days of the date you completed your registration form, it is important that you write to the following address or call (847) 688-6888.

Selective Service System
Registration Information Office
Post Office Box 94638
Palatine, IL 60064-4638

Verification of your registration or change of information can be done online at sss.gov.

Who would be drafted if the draft were reinstituted? Excellent question. According to the guidelines, men who will reach age 20 during the calendar year in which inductions occur would be the first group to be called. If more men are needed, the order of call would continue up to those who will reach age

21, then 22, and on up through age 25. The order of inductions within each age group would he determined by a lottery.

If you were ever selected for induction, you would be sent an "Order to Report for Induction" along with detailed instructions explaining where to report and what actions would be required on your part to fulfill this requirement. There are instances and circumstances that relieve you from going into the service if you file a claim for postponement or reclassification. If so, your induction would be delayed until a decision is made on whether the claim is accepted or denied. Some examples of the requirements to obtain a postponement or a reclassification are as follows:

Postponements: full-time college students who desire to finish their semester; full-time college students in their last academic year; high school students not yet 20 years old.

Reclassifications: men whose induction would create a hardship to his dependents; students studying for the ministry; ministers of religion; conscientious objectors (those who hold deep religious, moral, or ethical beliefs against participation in war. If the objection is to participate in combat military service only, one would be inducted to perform only non-combat military service; if the objection is to participate in all military service, in lieu of induction one would be ordered to perform civilian work contributing to the maintenance of the national health, safety, or interest as determined by the Director of Selective Service).

The moral of the story is, if you're in school, stay there until they give you your degree. You never know when a war may break out. God forbid, if it's right after the semester you decided that catching rays, drinking beer, and staying out all night was a better choice than going to class every now and then. Hello, Uncle Sam. By the way, those with college degrees are historically inducted as officers, whereas the others go in at the lowest rank. Education has all kinds of pay-offs.

CIGARETTES AND TOBACCO

Congratulations, you have turned 18 and can now legally possess tobacco products. As you are probably aware if you're reading this section, it is illegal in Texas to possess tobacco products if you are under 18. This can even impact your privilege to drive by causing license suspension in some instances. One other thing: Now that you are away from home and away from many constraints, this is a time you may form habits that may very well stick with you for many, many years. I don't have to tell you about tobacco's effects on health and certainly won't preach to you, but it is worth being said one more time: It is a habit that can become very difficult to kick and could ultimately kill you in a very unpleasant way.

DRIVER'S LICENSE

You must have a valid driver's license to drive, even a motorcycle or scooter. It also acts as proper identification.

New to Texas and over 18: Someone moving to Texas who has a valid driver license from his home state has 30 days to secure a Texas driver license. All first-time original applicants must visit a Texas Driver License office and present and do the following:

- Proof of identity, Social Security number and Texas vehicle registration and liability insurance, if you own a vehicle.
- Complete all required forms available at any Texas Driver License office.
- Pay the required fee and pass the vision exam.
- Appear for photograph and thumbprints; however, thumbprints are not included on the driver's license.
- If you have a VALID out-of-state license in your possession, please bring it to the driver license office to surrender.
- If you have an EXPIRED out-of-state license, you will be required to pass the written and driving exams, in addition to a vision test. (You must provide the vehicle for the road test).

Never had a license? If you are a new resident from out of the country or have never been licensed, it's the same as above, but if you do not have a Social Security number, you will need to complete a Social Security affidavit).

Renewal: You may renew your Texas driver's license up to one year before expiration. You can renew online, by telephone or by mail or in person at any Texas driver license office. You will be required to present proof of identity and proof of Social Security number, pass the vision exam and pay the required fees. If your Texas driver license has been expired for more than two years, you must appear in person at any Texas driver license office and apply as an original applicant.

Automatic driver's license suspensions, under 21: Minors get hit much harder for the same sort of suspensions than those who are over 21. Automatic suspensions occur when a minor is convicted for the offenses detailed in the section *Driver's License Suspensions in* Chapter 8, just like those over 21, but usually have a longer suspension period. There are also additional situations that apply only to those under 21, such as DWI (alcohol); intoxication assault; intoxication manslaughter; purchase, attempt to purchase, consumption or possession of alcohol by minor; misrepresentation of age by a minor; driving under the influence of alcohol, which means with any "detectable" amount of alcohol; and any drug offense. I almost forgot: There are usually other things you will have to do, like attend some sort of "educational" class before DPS will reinstate your driver's license.

CHAPTER 7
"LET'S PARTY"

IN THE IMMORTAL WORDS of the Beastie Boys, "You've got fight for your right to paaaaarrrrrrrrrrrrrrty." This is probably the chapter you have all turned to right off the bat, maybe even while standing in the bookstore. No matter, this may be the first time you have been truly on your own, with no curfew, no house rules, no household chores, and especially no parents keeping tabs on your whereabouts. This is definitely a time in your life where you are wanting to let your hair down, sow your oats, stretch your boundaries, go wild, or whatever you want to call it. I'm not here to tell you what to do or not do, but there are some things you need to know about the law that may affect when, where and what you are thinking about doing.

BEER, WINE AND COCKTAILS

Alcohol: Not often thought of as a drug, alcohol is classified as a sedative/hypnotic. It is also one of the most abused addictive substances by Americans, especially college students. Alcohol contributes to health problems resulting in death and complications more than any other drug and, notwithstanding its legalities, compulsive drinking in excess, commonly referred to as "binge drinking," has become a serious problem, especially on college campuses.

Ethyl alcohol, or ethanol, is the kind of alcohol you can drink and is produced by fermenting or distilling a clear, colorless liquid from various fruits, vegetables or grains. Alcoholic beverages get their color from the diluents, additives and by-products of fermentation and aging. The alcohol content varies depending on the type of alcoholic beverage you're drinking. Beer contains about 5 percent alcohol by volume (or 3.5 percent in light beer); wine is generally between 10 percent and 14 percent alcohol content; fortified wines such as sherry, port, and vermouth contain between 14 percent and 20 percent; and distilled spirits (whisky, vodka, rum, gin) are first fermented, then distilled to raise the alcohol content.

The effects of drinking do not depend on the type of alcoholic beverage, but rather on the amount of alcohol consumed over a period of time. Alcohol is rapidly absorbed into the bloodstream from the small intestine and less from the stomach and colon. The drinker's blood alcohol concentration depends on the amount consumed in a given time; the size, sex, body build, and metabolism of the person; and the type and amount of food in the stomach.

Once the alcohol has passed into the blood, food or beverage cannot diminish or interfere with its effects, however fruit sugar can shorten the duration of alcohol's effect by speeding up metabolism and thus its ultimate elimination from the blood. The metabolic rate of the average adult is about 8.5 grams of alcohol per hour (i.e. about two-thirds of a regular beer or about one shot per hour), but varies depending on the person's usual amount of drinking, physique, sex, liver size, and genetic factors.

Binge drinking has gained the attention of the media, school administrators, and the legal community in recent years. To magnify the problem, this trend is apparently popular with the younger and more inexperienced drinkers in our society, particularly on the college campus scene. Whether or not this is a new attitude of drinking or just a name given to something that has been done for decades is irrelevant. Extreme amounts of alcohol consumption can be a serious threat. It is possible for a person to consume so much alcohol in a short amount of time that the body goes into shock, and various bodily functions begin to shut down, basically poisoning oneself. Death is very real possibility in these circumstances. It is extremely important for anyone who sees someone consuming alcohol in an unusually large or quick fashion to step in assist that person with medical attention or close supervision.

Drinking heavily over a short period of time also usually results in a hangover: headache, nausea, shakiness, and sometimes vomiting, beginning from eight to 12 hours later. A hangover is due partly to poisoning by alcohol, the components of the drink, and partly to the body's reaction to withdrawal from alcohol. Although there are dozens of home remedies, there is no known effective cure.

Combining alcohol with other drugs can make their effects much stronger and more dangerous and even cause death. Alcohol should be avoided if you're taking tranquilizers, barbiturates, sleeping pills, or antihistamines (in cold, cough, and allergy remedies), among others.

Years of alcohol use can reveal the long-term effects, but may even appear after only months of heavy drinking. Chronic alcohol consumption can bring on serious negative physical and psychological problems that are potentially life-threatening, such as heart and liver disease or inflammation of the stomach, loss of appetite, vitamin deficiencies, infection, and generally a lowered immune system. Even moderate drinking can generate psychological dependence. This is seen in people who only drink under certain conditions, such as before and during certain social occasions, which usually suggests a type of dependence more for the craving of the alcohol's psychological effects, such as relaxation or anxiety relief, and not necessarily the intoxication itself.

Heavy drinkers begin to experience a physical dependence because their bodies have adapted to the alcohol and will suffer withdrawal symptoms if they suddenly stop drinking. Withdrawal symptoms range from jumpiness, sleeplessness, sweating and poor appetite, to tremors (the "shakes"), convulsions, hallucinations, and, sometimes, even death.

Legal drinking age: In the 1970s, generally speaking, the legal drinking age was 18. In the early '80 s, it was raised to 19 for a brief period and jumped to 21 a few years later. The federal government held the states hostage by threatening to withhold federal highway funds from states that didn't raise the legal drinking age to 21. Additionally, and in response to pressures by special interest groups such as Mothers Against Drunk Driving, state legislatures have continually tightened DWI laws, including lowering the legal blood/breath alcohol concentration. Although the drinking age is 21, a person can work in a bar or restaurant and serve alcohol at 18. A minor can legally consume an alcoholic beverage in Texas, but only if the minor is in the visible presence of the minor's adult parent, guardian, or spouse.

Underage drinking: This is probably one of the most-read portions of this book, as it is a subject near and dear to most college kids under 21. It is also an issue that university administrators, university police departments, and police departments continue to target. Why? The popular answer is that they are doing everyone a favor by vigorously enforcing the law and keeping the underage drinkers and the community safer. There may be some merit to these arguments, but another reason is that municipalities and courts have discovered that these types of prosecutions are a lucrative revenue source. I do not advocate or encourage underage drinking, but I also realize that it occurs and this book is intended to inform its readers, whatever their age.

For this section, we'll use a scenario and refer back to it as we go along.

Joe and the boys decide to do a little tailgating before the big game. They load up the truck with provisions: grill, food, chairs, TV, living room couch, several coolers, and well, yeah, some beer. They find a prime spot in the parking lot and set-up shop: cooking, eating, watching the other games, lounging around on their sofa, tossing the football around and enjoy the general merriments of game day, i.e. drinking. Friends begin to find their tailgate, the party starts to grow and the boys show the proper hospitality, feeding everyone and making their provisions available for everyone. Although the police generally give some leeway to such activity out in the open, they are still charged with keeping order and enforcing the law. Joe's crew observes some generally accepted policies of tailgating to avert or appease the police to avoid undue attention. The main problems that are gaining the most attention by the police patrolling the parking lots are:

- The boys have set-up a bar on the hood of one their cars and are mixing drinks from open liquor bottles.
- They are drinking bottled and canned beer out of the bottles and cans directly.
- They are disposing of their empties wherever they are when they finish them.
- One of the police officers approaches and starts to check IDs, BANG.

For a complete list of tailgating tips, see the *Where Can I Drink* section on "Tailgating Helpful Hints" later in this chapter.

Minor in possession (MIP): This is probably the most common underage drinking–related criminal offense. It is a Class C misdemeanor for a person under 21 to possess an alcoholic beverage. There are exceptions for employees of a licensee or permittee or for those in the visible presence of their adult parent, guardian, or spouse, or if they are working in a sting for the police.

The key to this offense and a successful prosecution is that the police officer must actually witness or see the minor in possession of the alcoholic beverage. Merely being near it at a party or in a car with other people is not sufficient.

Back to the tailgate. BANG, every underage person the officer sees holding a beer is probably going to get a ticket or maybe even be arrested if they are too intoxicated or give the officer trouble. The owners of the car where the liquor is, if they are underage, might also get a ticket for possession. Those underage drinkers who escape are those who escape detection. They are the ones who had their beverage in a nondescript plastic cup and the officers left them alone or they saw the officer approaching and disposed of their beverage in a stealthy manner. As for Joe and the guys who are over 21, they may be charged with furnishing alcohol to minors.

Consumption of alcohol by a minor (MIC): Obviously, a minor commits an offense if he consumes an alcoholic beverage, but not if he is in the visible presence of his adult parent, guardian, or spouse.

Similar to MIP, the key to a successful prosecution is direct evidence that the officer actually witnessed the consumption. In reality, police officers routinely ticket or even arrest minors they encounter who have the odor of alcohol on their breath. This is not the legal standard under the statute.

Back to the tailgate. BANG, again, every underage person the officers saw drinking a beer are probably going to get a ticket or maybe even arrested if they are too intoxicated or give the officer trouble. Everyone who is underage and smells like beer might get a ticket, but may have a defense to prosecution and should consult an attorney, as should anyone accused of a crime, even Class C misdemeanors like these. Why?

Punishments for underage drinking: Although relatively minor offenses are at the lowest end of the criminal justice system, the punishments for alcohol-related offenses by a minor continue to increase and multiple offenses can really start to affect your life, bank account and other important aspects of your lives.

Even a first-time conviction will require you to attend an alcohol awareness program, perform no less than 12 hours of community service, and result in the suspension of your driver's license for 30 days. In addition, you'll most likely pay a fine and court costs. Second offenders will have their driver's license suspended for 60 days, will perform between 20 and 40 hours of community service, be required to attend alcohol awareness classes, and pay a fine and court costs. Two prior convictions of these types of offenses not only increases the fine to $250 to $2,000, but you can also actually go to jail for up to 180 days, not to mention getting your driver's license suspended for 180 days.

Driving under the influence of alcohol: Although Joe is 21, he has driven several of his buddies to a hot party. A couple of his buddies are under age, but no worries, the party is cool and they have some beers from the keg and hang out with some chicks. The party is a success and, as it winds down, Joe is found passed out on the couch. His buddies collect him up, carry him to the car, fish his keys out of his pocket and strap him in. Since they all feel OK to drive, they flip to see who has to drive Joe's car. On the way home, the cops recognize Joe's car, broken taillight and all, and stop them. The officer sees Joe passed out and asks the others if they've been drinking. They all say "a couple of beers." This prompts the officer to have the driver step out of the car. He does and he looks fine, no stumbling, no slurred speech, or other signs of intoxication, but he does smell like beer. BANG! Although, no one is arrested for DWI, based on the smell of beer and the driver's admission that he had "a couple of beers," the officer tickets him for driving under the influence of alcohol (DUI), and the other underage passengers for consumption of alcohol by minor (MIC), all Class C misdemeanors.

DUI, as it's commonly referred, is committed if a minor operates a motor vehicle in a public place while having any detectable amount of alcohol in his system. Similar to a DWI, refusal to take a breath test carries an administrative license suspension of 30 days, but can be contested in an administrative hearing. Like other offenses, punishments increase with prior offenses. A third offense is punishable by up to 180 days in jail, a fine between $500 and $2,000; and other driver's license suspension issues.

Texas Alcoholic Beverage Commission (TABC): Agents from TABC are peace officers, just like a sheriff or a city policeman, but they have no more authority to search and arrest than any other peace officer and have no more authority under the law to enter and search a private residence and arrest an occupant on "minor in possession" (MIP) charges.

An officer may knock on the door and ask permission to conduct a search, but "suspicion" alone does not give him the authority to enter or search a private home.

If a police officer is invited into a private home or if the officer's presence in the home is authorized in some manner and the officer sees a crime committed, he may make an arrest for any offense committed in his presence, including MIP.

A warrant to search a home for a specific item of contraband or evidence of a crime requires an affidavit stating the facts supporting the probable cause, but to search for an illicit can of beer or other Texas Alcoholic Beverage Code violations, affidavits from two credible persons are required.

Any peace officer (including TABC agents) may search a premise covered by a license or permit to serve alcohol without a search warrant.

When can I buy?

Beer, wine and cocktails: From 7 a.m. until midnight except Sundays. On Sundays, you can buy beer from midnight to 1 a.m., from noon to midnight, and from 10 a.m. to noon if the beer is served with food. There are other late hour and on-premises license holder exceptions that allow clubs and other similar places to sell until 2 a.m.

Liquor: From 10 a.m. to 9 p.m., except Sundays, Thanksgiving, Christmas and New Year's Day. When these holidays fall on a Sunday, the sale of liquor is also prohibited on the following Monday.

Where can I drink?

At home: Anytime you want, so long as it is not in a public place.

Public places: Anytime except between 1:15 a.m. and noon on Sundays and 12:15 a.m. and 7 a.m. any other day.

Bars and clubs: These places usually hold licenses that make them "extended hours areas," which extend the public place hours on these premises. This allows you to drink your drinks after closing time at the club for 15 minutes, extending the allowable consumption period to 2:15 a.m. Basically, if you can buy it, you've got at least 15 minutes to suck it down. Otherwise it is a Class C misdemeanor.

Tailgating and concerts: I fondly refer to this as the "Texan Tailgating Law." As you can see above, if you are a fan of professional football, drinking before a noon game on Sunday can be problematic. Being a devoted Houston Texan fan and avid tailgater, this posed a problem for my crew during the Texans' first two seasons. However, in January 2004 an exception to the hours of consumption on Sunday was enacted, allowing a person to begin consuming alcoholic beverages at a sports venue (including the parking lot) at 10 a.m. This law does not totally remedy the problem, because the gates open at 8 a.m., but it's a start. The Legislature has recently expanded this to include festivals, fairs and concerts.

Identification

Failure To Identify: While at a big party, the cops arrive and shut down the scene. They instruct everyone to leave, but on your way out (and although you have done absolutely nothing), the officer stops you and asks you for ID. Not only because you are underage, but you feel you are being singled out and hassled, you decide to refuse the officer's request. You know you don't have to carry a driver's license or other ID if you're not driving, so you refuse, just to spite the officer. If you've just been detained, not arrested, you don't have to give them squat, but refusing to identify might cause them to arrest you anyway and take you downtown so they can determine who you really are. If this happens, you still won't be charged with failing to carry ID, because there is no such crime.

If you've been arrested, you have to give your name, address, and date of birth to a police officer who requests it. The police will ask you for a lot more than this, but these three items are all you're legally required to give them. If you refuse to do so, you will probably be charged with the Class C misdemeanor offense of failure to identify.

Instead of refusing altogether, you tell him you don't have any ID and tell him that your name is Mickey Mouse, from Orlando, Florida. BANG, you're under arrest for giving a false or fictitious name, residence address, or date of birth. If the peace officer has lawfully arrested or detained you or has good cause to believe you are a witness to a criminal offense, this is a Class B misdemeanor.

Realizing that you have a warrant for your arrest from the speeding ticket you ignored last semester, you either refuse to give the ID information or give false info. The offense you may be charged with is raised one level because of the warrant. You were "a fugitive from justice" when you committed the offense.

Fake ID: You didn't go see Crazy Lola (see Chapter 13), but you have started a little collection of IDs from older brothers and friends for use on occasion to get into clubs and such. When you are stopped one night and as you're getting your real ID out, several others accidentally fall on the ground. BANG, you are arrested for possessing multiple IDs.

It is illegal to possess more than one valid driver's license or provide a false name, address, make a false statement or commit fraud when applying for an original, renewal or duplicate driver's license. It is also illegal to lend a driver's license or permit someone nor can you display or represent as your own a driver's license not issued to you. These offenses are misdemeanors.

This time the cops bust the party, you are ready, you went to see Crazy Lola (refer to Chapter 13) and got one of her famous and perfect fake IDs, complete with your own picture, name, address and date of birth, with two years added to boot. You flip the ID to the cop and he then runs the info. He discovers the discrepancy between your ID and the state's database and investigates further. BANG, BANG, you are under arrest for tampering with a government record. It's a Class A misdemeanor, unless the intent is to defraud or harm another, in which event the offense is a state jail felony.

DWI: Driving While Intoxicated (DWI) is the most frequently prosecuted misdemeanor offense in the state of Texas and probably nationwide. It is also has some of the most damaging and far-reaching ramifications to a citizen's everyday life if convicted. The safest policy, legalities aside, is don't drink and drive. Take a cab or walk. That being said, it is not illegal in Texas to drink and then drive. It is illegal for a driver and passengers to consume alcoholic beverages or have an open container of an alcoholic beverage in the vehicle. What gets you in trouble is when you are driving after drinking so much that you are intoxicated. In Texas, it is illegal to operate a motor vehicle in a public place with a blood/breath alcohol concentration of .08 or higher or while having lost the normal use of one's mental or physical faculties by the introduction of alcohol (or other substance). That is a long, but important definition of DWI law in Texas.

It is extremely important to try and prevent the first DWI conviction. Many people make the mistake of failing to defend themselves in a first offense DWI because first offenders are typically offered a relatively light punishment involving probation. They're under the assumption that they do not intend to ever place themselves in a position of being charged a second time. Unfortunately, they do not truly realize that because of the extremely subjective nature of the charge (i.e. the officer's opinion that someone is intoxicated), if an officer smells an odor of an alcoholic beverage and then runs the driver's license, discovering the prior DWI, that person's chance of being arrested and charged with DWI again is extremely high.

Legally intoxicated: What is intoxicated? In Texas, it is having a blood/breath alcohol concentration of .08 or higher or loss of the normal use of one's mental or physical faculties by the introduction of alcohol (or other substance/drug) into one's body.

A public place is just about everywhere you can drive a car or truck except maybe on property that is not open to the public (i.e. ranch land, hunting leases, private roads). This includes just about everywhere else, including parking lots and driveways.

A motor vehicle is everything you think it probably would be: cars, trucks, motorcycles, dune buggies, tractors, trolleys, scooters, mopeds, Vespas. If it has a motor, it is probably considered a motor vehicle, even a golf cart. This even includes boats and personal watercrafts.

Operating means driving, but it also includes situations where people have been found in the driver's seat after an accident and even passed out at traffic lights with the foot on the brake. Any affirmative act, such as turning the key or siting behind the wheel may qualify. This is not an area of distinction you truly want to fool with.

So you have been at a bar or party, it's late at night and you are now driving home. Whether you are snot-slinging drunk, a little buzzed or just had "two or three beers" you need to know how to conduct yourself if stopped by a police officer and what rights you have. If you are stopped you must present a valid Texas driver's license, proof of insurance and you must comply with the officer's requests, such as getting out of the car, standing where you are directed and following the officer's commands concerning arrest. Other than that, you really don't have to do much else. You do not have to answer any questions, you do not have to take any field sobriety tests and you do not have to take a breathalyzer test or submit blood.

Remember, the officer on the street is always concerned for his own safety, so don't give him any reason to be apprehensive or nervous. No furtive movements or aggressive gestures or language. Remember that anything you do can be used to prosecute you and may even be on videotape. Questions by the officer and the standardized field sobriety tasks are designed to gather evidence against you in an attempt to prosecute and convict you. Unfortunately, an officer's perceptions can be skewed or affected by his personal views or interests. If you decide to answer questions and take tests, do not be surprised that they're used as evidence to prosecute you. Additionally, don't be surprised if the officer's testimony about what you said or how you performed on the field sobriety test is not what you remember.

Stupid human tricks – roadside tests: Officers use field sobriety tests on drivers they suspect are intoxicated. The great likelihood is that if an officer is asking you to take a test, he has already decided that you are intoxicated and he is just trying to confirm and further support this opinion. These tests are designed to detect minor motor skill mistakes and lack of attentiveness, all interpreted as "loss of normal use of mental and/or physical faculties." The interpretations of the performance of these exercises are can be interpreted in a number of ways. The truth is that there really isn't a "passing" grade.

You must make your own decision whether to take these "tests" based upon what you think is in your best interest, realizing that the entire battery of "tests" to be performed are really an exercise in evidence collection to ultimately convict you of DWI. These "tests" do not give credit for the citizen's adequate performance, only the incorrect portions or "mistakes" are evaluated and considered as "clues" or "signs" of intoxication.

The tests that are most commonly administered are:

The Horizontal Gaze Nystagumus Test (HGN), which is when an officer asks the person to follow a pen or finger from side to side with his eyes. The officer is looking for a twitching of the eye that suggests the presence of alcohol that arguably exacerbates this naturally occurring and ever-present condition.

The "Walk and Turn" is a "divided attention test" where an officer asks a person to take nine steps on a line heel to toe with arms at his side. The officer also asks the person to stand in an awkward position while giving him difficult instructions.

"One Leg Stand." The subject must stand on one leg, with the other extended approximately six inches from the ground, arms at his side and count to 30. Try it. It's hard.

Rhomberg Test. The subject stands with his head back and estimates (in his head) 30 seconds. Studies have shown that humans cannot internally keep time, much less accurately estimate 30 seconds. The officer is also watching to see if you sway during this "test." Additionally, tilting of the head disrupts the inner-ear function, which controls balance.

Nose Touch. The officer asks the person to tilt his head back, close his eyes and touch his nose. There is no academic or scientific support for this test.

Many of the tests and instructions are similar to the childhood game of "Simon Says," which is designed to "trick" the person into doing something he didn't really mean to do. The testimony at trial will be that these mistakes are all signs of intoxication and demonstrate that you lost the normal use of your mental or physical faculties.

The officer's observations and testing interpretation represents the vast majority of evidence presented in DWI trials. It is rare that an officer administers the field sobriety test and then lets someone get back in the car and drive home. If it has happened to you, you are lucky. One thing that seems to always be reported is that the officers become agitated or increasingly threatening when a citizen advices them that they are not going to submit to any testing. Just remember, it is your right to refuse. We will talk about license suspensions and whether or not to take a breath test a little later, but remember any and all statements you make will probably be used against you. Just remember, there is no "passing" grade, merely observations that indicate loss of mental or physical faculties, so don't think you will ever "pass" the field sobriety tests.

Lastly, the officer will be asking you some questions. What questions might be asked of you?

- Where are you going?
- Where have you been?
- What time is it?
- Have you been drinking?
- How much?
- May I search your vehicle?

All of these seem quite harmless, but each have the potential to being very damaging if presented in court the right way. Refer to Chapter 2 regarding your legal rights, especially the right to remain silent. You do not have to answer any questions, other than identification and insurance, nor do any tests.

Classic signs of intoxication: What are the "classic signs of intoxication" that are found in almost every police officer's report?

- Weaving inside the lines.
- Driving to fast, driving too slow.
- Driving without your lights on.
- Braked too late.
- Making a wide turn.
- Running a stop sign or light.
- Blood-shot and glassy eyes.
- Slurred or slow speech.
- "Mush mouthed."
- Unsteady on feet.
- Unsure balance.
- Smell of alcohol on breath or person.
- Leaned on car for balance.

The crime of DWI: Every other offense that is probated in the state of Texas (murder, rape, incest with a barnyard animal just to name a few) cannot be used to enhance punishment of subsequent charges, with one notable exception: DWI.

DWI cannot be disposed of through deferred adjudication. A first conviction is a Class B misdemeanor, a second is a Class A misdemeanor and a third is a third-degree felony, with the very real potential of time in prison.

DWI is also one of the very few crimes that is based solely upon another person's opinion rather than definitive evidence. Whether someone has loss the normal use of their mental or physical faculties is one of opinion, therefore several different people may have completely different opinions regarding the person's guilt.

If you cause an accident while intoxicated and someone suffers serious bodily injury or, God forbid, dies, then the offense can be elevated to intoxication assault or intoxication manslaughter, second- and first-degree felonies. It's also a felony if there is a child in the car while the driver is intoxicated.

A DWI conviction carries a lot of extra baggage, such as mandatory license suspensions in certain situations, mandatory attendance of alcohol education classes, installation of an interlock device, not to mention insurance headaches and a $1,000 minimum annual "surcharge" assessment for license renewal for three years.

Should I blow? Unless I have had absolutely no alcohol in more than 24 hours, I would not take the test. Based upon my experiences in trial, consultations with experts in various medical, scientific and legal fields of study, I do not feel that the devices are reliable enough to accurately detect blood-alcohol levels based upon a breath sample sufficient to convince me to take one. (See *Blow and Go/The Interlock Device* section below for more info.)

A blood test is a much more accurate test, but it too has some margin for error. If you decide to submit to a test, you may ask for a blood test but they must comply only if you can arrange for a person certified to do so within a very short period of time and usually in the middle of the night. It usually is not a viable option.

What happens if I blow or give blood? If you submit to a breath/blood test and it shows a level of 0.08 or greater, you will be charged with DWI. The prosecuting attorney will use the result as extremely reliable evidence, proving his case "beyond a reasonable doubt." Your license will also probably be suspended for 90 days for a first time failure. The suspension periods increase with subsequent "alcohol contacts." The suspension is not automatic as explained below in the *How Will This Affect My Driver's License* section.

If you pass the test, it is important to understand that this will not guarantee you are just let go and not charged with DWI. If you are under the limit, but show some alcohol consumption, the state may simply argue that it only shows that you were under the limit when you took the test, and because of absorption and elimination, your blood-alcohol level was higher when you were driving earlier. If you pass without any alcohol detected, law enforcement will then usually call in a drug recognition expert who will evaluate you and determine that you are under the influence of an "unknown drug," most likely a central nervous system depressant, which has caused the loss of normal use of mental or physical faculties. The lack of a presence of alcohol merely supports their subjective opinion they formed based on your performance of the "field sobriety tests" given earlier.

What happens if I don't? If you refuse the test, your license may be suspended for 180 days and your refusal may be used against you. This suspension is not "automatic" as believed and as stated by law enforcement officers. But the possibility exists if after you request a hearing, the DPS adequately proves the necessary elements to support the suspension, but is definitely not "automatic." The most important advantage your refusal provides is that the state will have to rely on the "loss of normal use" definition of intoxication alone and will not have "scientific" evidence (i.e. breath test) supporting the police officer's subjective opinion.

Can they make me do it? Yes and no. Not the breath test. But it is another story when it comes to blood.

The state can forcibly extract blood from someone, but it usually requires a warrant signed by a judge. It can also draw blood when there has been an accident where the driver has been arrested for DWI AND the driver's automobile was involved in an accident caused by the driver being intoxicated AND the officer reasonably believes a person has died or will die as a result of the accident.

Otherwise your consent is required for any and all testing, whether blood, breath or urine. Many times, where a driver suspected of DWI is taken to the hospital for minor treatment, the driver's medical records are regularly subpoenaed by the district attorney's office to see if the hospital did any blood tests in the normal course of treatment that indicates alcohol or drug levels. If so, they then attempt to use those results as evidence in trial.

Blood testing and "no refusal": It is becoming more fashionable and politically popular for district attorneys to promote the concept of "no refusal" by marketing and publicizing "no refusal weekends" during certain holidays or weekends (New Year's, Memorial Day, July Fourth, Labor Day). Some have gone to even calling themselves "no refusal counties." All this really means is that they have arranged for judges to be on call to facilitate "blood warrants." The fact that they call it "no refusal weekend" or "no refusal county" or "no refusal anything" does not change the fact that without your consent and voluntary submission, they must get a warrant, reviewed for probable cause and signed by a judge to make you submit a sample of blood. It is still your right to refuse their request and something I recommend any citizen should consider for a variety of reasons. There are some constitutional protections built in to the warrant process, and the scientific testing results may be arguably and potentially more reliable compared to the breath testing alternative.

If a warrant has been issued and you forcibly resist in the blood sample extraction process, they are usually authorized to restrain you to facilitate the forcible extraction of blood.

How will this affect my driver's license? That depends on your particular case and the ultimate disposition. License suspensions from either a refusal to take or failing a breath/blood test is totally separate from the DWI prosecution. It is an administrative license revocation pursued through the administrative law function of the state Office of Administrative Hearings. The only instance where the outcome of a criminal prosecution affects an ALR license suspension is when a jury acquits the person charged or the case is dismissed on a breath test failure case. In that instance, the license suspension can be rescinded, but other dispositions of a DWI prosecution generally do not affect an ALR suspension.

A first-time DWI conviction carries a one-year suspension (no suspension if there is probation). All subsequent convictions will result in license suspension, with the length depending on prior record and suspensions.

Your license will probably be confiscated if you either blow and fail or refuse. If not and your license is suspended or revoked for any reason, DPS may require you to surrender it to DPS. Failure to surrender the license is a Class B misdemeanor.

"Blow and go"/the interlock device: Texas law allows a court to order installation of an ignition interlock device on the vehicles of people who have been convicted of and placed on probation for DWI and other offenses, as a condition of bond, and as a condition of granting an occupational driver's license. Texas law requires that courts must order installation of an ignition interlock device on vehicles driven by someone arrested and charged with a second DWI as a condition of their bond.

There are several manufacturers of ignition interlock devices, which are breath-alcohol analyzers connected to the vehicle's ignition system. Before the car's is started, the driver must first blow a breath sample into the device, which then measures the alcohol concentration in the breath and prevents starting if the device detects a certain amount of alcohol in the driver's breath. Once the car is started, a re-test is required after a certain period of time. All test results, starts and "lock outs" are recorded on the device's internal hard drive. These records are made available to the courts for review. This has also become a little revenue source, as only certain companies are "approved" by the courts and therefore profit from the orders.

What's the problem? There is a great amount of debate over the reliability of these types of machines. Prosecutors and law enforcement have taken the position that they are extremely accurate and therefore should be trusted completely; defense attorneys, those accused and others, including scientists and researchers, have differing views.

Breath analyzers (Breathalyzer, Intoxilyzer, Alcosensor, Alcoscan and BAC Datamaster are common brand names) don't actually test blood alcohol concentration, which requires the analysis of a blood sample. Instead, these machines estimate blood-alcohol concentration indirectly through an analysis of the person's breath. A major problem with some of the machines used by law enforcement and especially these "blow and go" devices is that they not only detect the ethyl alcohol (or ethanol) found in alcoholic beverages, but also similar molecular structures that are found in other substances, thus indicating a presence of alcohol when there is none. According to the National Highway Traffic Safety Administration, even dieters and diabetics can have abnormally high acetone levels in their breath, which is just one of the substances referred to above. Other common substances have been reported to affect these machines, such as dirt and moisture; blood or vomit; tobacco smoke; contact with and breathing the fumes of gasoline, paint and cleaning fluids; residual alcohol from mouthwashes and other oral cleansers; electrical interference from cell phones and police radios; and even the ambient temperature of the surrounding air and the body temperature of the subject.

The long and the short of it is that these machines attempt to deduce and measure the alcohol amount in the blood by looking at the breath. You must decide what is reliable and what is or is not in your best interest.

DWI conviction "surcharge" – the forgotten baggage: With every DWI conviction comes an extra hidden bonus that is often overlooked. Anyone who has a DWI conviction is assessed an annual surcharge by the Texas Department of Public Safety for three years. This "surcharge" must be paid to DPS to renew a driver's license each of those three years. Non-payment results in a driver's license suspension that will not be lifted until the payment is made. A grand total of $3,000 for a first offense DWI conviction, no matter the actual sentence assessed. Second convictions and cases with blood/breath results over 0.15 are $1,500 per year and they go up from there.

Public intoxication: The ever-popular offense of public intoxication is used to great extent by the authorities to control rowdiness and belligerent people they encounter during the course of their patrol. It is very often abused and gives an unethical officer an extremely subjective "legal" reason to arrest you if he wishes. It is a subjective decision by the officer whether you are committing the offense of public intoxication, so how you act and respond to an officer has a great deal of importance to your freedom at that time.

Let's say you have been out with some friends and y'all decide to drop by the late-night diner for breakfast. You have had a couple of pops at the bar earlier but feel fine. The police drop in for a cup of coffee and while they are there, for whatever reason — probably your friends' loud discussion about politics or religion, as well as the occasional curse word — they notice your group. After settling up, you leave. No harm done. As you are walking down the sidewalk, the police officers stop and ask for some ID. You produce your ID, but make a harmless comment or sarcastic remark that does not please the officer. He smells beer on your breath or asks "have you been drinking?" You reply, "Yes, a couple of beers."

This is where things turn bad. Under Texas law, if the officer subjectively believes that you are intoxicated, not necessarily by the legal standard for DWI, but "to the degree that you may endanger yourself or another," he is legally authorized to arrest for public intoxication, a Class C misdemeanor. If you are under 21, you face other potential problems. Nonetheless, you have to spend the night in jail.

The same thing applies to parties, gatherings, concerts and festivals. Don't make the mistake of arguing with the officer or relying on what is or is not a "public place" under the law. For your own decision-making purposes, assume wherever you are, unless it's in your own home, you are in a "public place" and act accordingly.

Girls gone wild. Not being of the female persuasion, I cannot personally attest to the effect that the sight of cameras, swimsuit contests, and cheap plastic beads actually have on women.

But having witnessed this phenomenon throughout the U.S. and the world, apparently these sights can turn normally demure, well-behaved young women into fanatic exhibitionists. I make a little joke and while I certainly didn't mind the effect, I have given the subject some thought and decided to include this section for the ladies.

Joe's sister, Sissy, who is remarkably similar to Joe and shares many of the same gene-pool characteristics, heads down to Padre for spring break, right on the heels of a trip to Bourbon Street during Mardi Gras. They find the party scene on Padre very similar: cheap beer, public urination, mobs of alcohol-soaked kids, even bead throwing, or rather, catching, popularly known as "bead-baiting," which they had become quite adept at. Sissy and her girls are occasionally "coaxed" into showing their goods after they have had a few, errr 10 beers and a few shots. Fortunately none of the girls has been busted by the cops for her escapades and public bearing of breasts, so they figure just some good clean fun and "sowing some wild oats." Later that semester, Sissy happens upon some guys in the frat house watching a video of girls exposing themselves at Spring Break. To her shock, she happens to see her whole gang shaking their goods on the beach last Spring Break. Now someone is not only showing it to the world over and over, but they are also making tons of money doing so.

Naïve maybe, but it has apparently surprised some that have filed lawsuits challenging the use, sale and distribution of these videos. A 25-year-old former swimsuit model in Florida discovered she was a *Girl Gone Wild – Sexy Sorority Sweetheart* and filed a lawsuit claiming to have been an unwitting and unwilling participant by the use of her likeness without permission. She claimed the video has subjected her to ridicule and embarrassment. Others have tried also, to no avail.

If you don't know, there are people who send camera crews to wander the beaches and streets of spring break, Mardi Gras and campus parties looking for opportunities to record spontaneous and usually drunken young women flashing their breasts. These videos are marketed on the Internet and in late-night TV infomercials. Now for the kicker, it's all legal.

Do you have a right to privacy in public areas? Generally speaking, NO! (see Chapter 5). Remember, no matter how many beers, shots and Bourbon Street hurricanes you guzzle down, if you're not careful, you may be tomorrow's Internet queen.

Mardi Gras bead-baiting ("show your tits"): While Joe and the guys were in New Orleans for Mardi Gras, they enjoyed the pastime of "bead-baiting" the women. So the next year, Joe and the boys bring this tradition home to spring break. From the balcony of their hotel room overlooking the South Padre Island beach, the boys are producing their own video of the girls going wild below by throwing them beads for their effort. Unfortunately, the cops on Padre Island don't look the other way like they do in New Orleans. BANG, the girls are busted for indecent exposure. Unfortunately, one of the girls Joe was coaxing into "showing her tits," as it's called, turns out to be 16. BANG, Joe and the boys are arrested for sexual performance of a child, a second-degree felony.

Although this crime is intended to prevent the exploitation of children, typically child pornography, it is easy to see a situation where a zealous D.A. may charge Joe and the guys with this offense. What has happened below Joe's hotel balcony is "sexual conduct," which includes exhibition of the female breast below the top of the areola.

DRUGS ... THAT INCLUDES MARIJUANA

Drugs have been a right of passage and a part of America's youth, collegiate campuses and the counter-culture since the 1960s. The "drug war" was declared in the 1980s to confront the perceived problems associated with the drug trade, with much stiffer sentences through federal sentencing guidelines. The Texas Health and Safety Code deals with almost all of the major drug offense language and, by and large, the severity of the offense depends on what it is and how much is possessed, manufactured or delivered.

Marijuana: With the advent of legalization in other states and the debate over de-criminalization and medical marijuana, some of you may not realize that "pot" or "weed" is illegal. Notwithstanding whether you think it should be legalized or not, in the state of Texas, it is a crime to possess a usable amount of marijuana. If it is less than four ounces, then it is considered a misdemeanor (up to two ounces is a Class B misdemeanor and two to four ounces is a Class A). It becomes a state jail felony if the amount is between four ounces and five pounds, a third-degree felony if the amount is over five pounds but under 50. Larger amounts escalate upwards to 99 years as potential punishments. The manufacture, delivery or intent to deliver any amount over a quarter of an ounce is a felony.

Granted, public opinions are changing rapidly and some jurisdictions have exercised the recognized authority to "cite and release" small possession encounters. This basically means they choose to issue a ticket, setting a court date and avoiding the initial on-scene arrest. But this is still the minority view within law enforcement.

Felony brownies — hash oil / keef: Substances that are resin extracts or derivatives of marijuana containing concentrated amounts of THC have become more prevalent. However they carry greater criminal exposure. Some of these substances are commonly referred to as hashish, hash oil, honey oil and keef. Possession of these substances in any amount are felony offenses. The tricky part is that while the raw substance's criminal offense level is based entirely on its weight, if the material is combined with other legal items, the combined weight is the basis for the offense.

For instance, Joe goes skiing in Colorado for spring break. He visits a couple of legal marijuana dispensaries and purchases marijuana and some tasty gluten-free, vegan snacks that also contain the good stuff. Joe decides to bring back some of the healthy brownies for his vegan girlfriend and even a small amount of weed that he did not finish smoking on the slopes. While cruising back through West Texas, he is stopped for speeding. The smell of the previously smoked weed and Joe's laid-back attitude gives the cops some reasonable suspicion of illegal possession. They conduct a search and BANG, Joe picks up not only a misdemeanor charge for possession of marijuana, but the brownies are a felony. In fact, when the cops weigh the brownies, they weigh almost two pounds, which makes Joe's felony charge a very serious one.

Although there are small amounts of THC contained in the brownies, all the other ingredients add up and are considered in the total weight. While illogical, that is the state of the law. Secondly, just because it is legal in one state does not make it legal in another.

Controlled substances (ecstasy, cocaine, GHB, mushrooms, etc.): Possession of these substances and others in the Penalty Groups 1-4 of the Texas Health and Safety Code are illegal without a valid prescription. The severity of the offense depends on the penalty group and how much is possessed. Here is the general range:

- Less than one gram (any detectable amount): state jail felony.
- One to four grams: third-degree felony.
- Four to 200 grams: second-degree felony.
- 200 to 400 grams: first-degree felony.
- More than 400 grams: 10 years to life.

LSD: Lysergic acid diethylamide, more commonly referred to as "acid," is listed in its own "special" schedule because of the unusual way it is distributed (i.e. on little slips of paper or cards legally referred to as "abuse units," known on the street as a "dose" or "hit").

- Less than 20 units: state jail felony.
- 20-80 units: third-degree felony.
- 80 to 4,000 units: second-degree feloy.
- 4,000-8,000 units: first-degree felony

- More than 8,000 units: 15 years to a life.

Steroids: Anabolic steroids have been used for years by athletes to gain mass and muscle. A side effect of the drug war spawned new concerns about steroids in the late 1980s, ultimately resulting in federal and state laws classifying many of these as controlled substances. I'm certainly not going to preach about the health-related dangers of these substances or their reported side effects, but rather the legal consequences you may face if you decide to use or sell them. The safest choice, both legally and medically, is to stay clean and train drug-free. The substances that have been outlawed are found in Penalty Group 3 and possession of these substances are classified as:

- Less than 28 grams: Class B misdemeanor.
- 28 to 200 grams: third-degree felony.
- 200 to 400 grams: second-degree felony.
- More than 400 grams: Five years to life.

Manufacture or delivery: If you are "dealing," the offense level is generally raised a notch for the amount possessed, except the lowest levels remain the same and the higher-end minimum prison sentences are increased. Intent to deliver may be proved by the way the drugs are packaged or by an amount that would not be reasonable for personal use.

Dangerous drugs: A "dangerous drug" is basically a prescription drug. Some popular drugs that usually fall into this category and are regularly prosecuted are Adderrall, Darvocet, Haldol, Oxycontin, Ritalin, and Valium.

Let's say you are complaining that your knee hurts from a game of touch football. One of your buddies offers some of his pain medicine from when he had his wisdom teeth pulled. You take one and put the rest in the console of your car and forget about them. One night, months later, you're stopped for speeding and arrested for that outstanding ticket we talked about earlier. During the inventory search of your car they find those forgotten pills. BANG, you're under arrest for possessing a dangerous drug, a Class A misdemeanor. Your buddy's offer to give you the pills and the delivery is technically a state jail felony.

Drug-free zones: Texas and other states have made certain places especially problematic for the possession of illegal drugs. Let's say you are living on campus and it's just another day in the life, when you roll out of the sack, flick on the tube and spark up a bowl. You and your roommate are just hanging, when the knock on the door comes. You scramble to hide the bong, spray some air freshener and open the door to find the campus police standing there. After their initial interrogation, they search your room and find the bong and your stash. BANG, you and your roommate are taken into custody. Depending how much weed there is controls the severity of the charge, but more important, since you are in possession in a "drug free zone," the level of offense may be raised a level, making the charge much more severe than you ever thought possible.

The following are drug-free zones:

- Institutions of higher education, which means any public or private technical institute, junior college, senior college or university, medical or dental unit, or other agency of higher education.
- Playgrounds.
- Schools and day-care centers.
- Video arcades.
- Youth centers.
- Playgrounds.
- School buses.
- Within 1,000 feet of property owned or leased by institutions of higher learning, youth centers or playgrounds, and within 300 feet of public swimming pools or video arcades.

Next time you think about sparking one up at the secluded playground or any other place that you think may be a "drug-free zone," remember the penalties go up if you're caught in those places.

Drug paraphernalia: Possession of a bong, pipe, dugout, or whatever you're thinking about is a Class C misdemeanor for a first time offense. If you tried to give the paraphernalia to someone under 18 or to someone who was going to use it to grow, manufacture or deliver illegal drugs, it is a state jail felony.

Drug testing: Drug testing has become a regular course of policy in the workplace for new hires and continued employment. Millions of people are required to submit to drug tests. While the constitutionality of these policies and their violation of their Fourth and Fifth Amendment rights continue to be debated, drug testing could reach into the admission and attendance process of some colleges.

The practice of masking or trying to "fool" the tests has become big business. But it is against the law in Texas to falsify drug test results.

"LET'S HAVE A PARTY"

That's how it usually starts. It always sounds like an excellent idea, but sometimes the party can cause some headaches for the hostess. Obviously, when you open your home, either to friends or the campus in general for an "open" party, your home is at risk. Sometimes people can act a little more free with your house and furnishings than they might at their own home. Granted, you don't want to be the party wrecker, but a little preparation may prevent some problems later. If you are going to have people in and out of your house or apartment, you may want to hide anything that you don't want walking off or accidentally getting broken. Don't get me wrong, I'm not paranoid, but sometimes people you don't know may show up, and you don't want to watch out for everyone and everything.

Noise and music: One man's music is another man's noise. No matter the artistic attributes and entertainment value of the "music," most cities and towns have some form of noise ordinances. These rules are extremely subjective and are usually in place as a tool the authorities use to discourage loud music and wild parties. To their credit, most police agencies have a policy of warning the owners at least once before they write a ticket for the Class C offense. After that and the noise continues, the police may take the position that it is a breach of the peace and start arresting people to control the situation. The best bet is to try to keep it low enough that they don't ever come. If they do, turn it down and hopefully they will go away. Two common offenses charged in these situations are a Class C misdemeanor of noise and disorderly conduct, which is a catch-all and convenient way for the cops to keep order.

The neighbors. Another little thing that may keep the cops from coming early or even at all is to invite the neighbors, or at least give them a day or two notice that you may be having a soirée. Either they will join in the revelry or possibly find other plans that take them out and away from the loud music, crowd and traffic.

The police are at the front door. It is up to you to be calm and polite. Refer to the earlier chapters regarding Search and Seizure and Some Good Advice Concerning the Police, as well as your legal rights and you should do just fine. Sometimes, you are going to have to break up the party yourself and move on. If this happens, always be careful that the police are not just waiting around the corner or down the road to stop you or your guests, so don't give them any reason or opportunity to do so.

Providing the alcohol

Civil liability: It is illegal to provide, sell, or serve an alcoholic drink to an "obviously intoxicated" person. It makes the provider potentially liable for any injury caused by the "obviously intoxicated" customer.

This law only applies to liquor license holders, such as nightclubs, bars, convenience stores, and grocery stores, not private individuals. It is most commonly used to sue a bar, club or store that served or sold alcohol to someone who then injured or killed someone.

This sounds like it would be easy to prove, but proving that the person who served the drinks knew the person was "obviously intoxicated" and "presented a clear danger to himself or others" when served is harder than it may first appear. That being said, taking this law to the extreme can lead to some unique possibilities.

For instance, Joe and his buddy, Buddy, go out for a night of drinking. After a couple or 10 beers at a watering hole, the two have a disagreement over the tab and end up in a fight in the parking lot. Joe gets the best of Buddy and knocks three of his teeth out. BANG, Buddy may have some cause to sue the bar for his teeth if he can demonstrate that the bar served Joe when he was "obviously intoxicated" AND that they knew he was a "clear danger to Buddy" AND Joe's intoxication was the proximate cause of Buddy's bloody chicklets laying in the parking lot. This example does not even consider Buddy's contributory negligence that may mitigate or destroy his claim, but is merely an extreme example. This may also spill over into situations involving minors.

Let's say Buddy is underage and then gets into his truck and ultimately hits a telephone pole and knocks the rest of his teeth out. BANG, he may even be able to successfully sue the bar for the injuries he causes himself. Some states, not Texas, even extend this liability to serving "habitually intoxicated" people. Let's say Buddy's uncle, Cooter Brown, who everyone knows is always drunk, comes in for a drink every day and has a few. Over time, Uncle Cooter has squandered the family fortune and because of his drunkenness, the family business also goes under. The family may even be able to argue that the bar serving him "caused" Uncle Cooter to piss away his family's fortunes. These are extreme cases, but are within the realm of possibilities, considering the evolving legal and social landscape over recent years.

Known as Texas' Dram Shop law, it does not apply to party guests or social occasions where they are not sold the drinks. That's not to say absolutely no liability may come from the kegger Joe has almost every Friday night, such as allowing underage people to drink. But it won't be under the Dram Shop law for their actions later. Although a party host may not have this legal liability, the best practice is to make sure intoxicated guests don't try something foolish, like drive. Take control and have a friend, cab or Uber take them home, just for safe measure.

Criminal liability: This is where things get tricky and is really the major concern when throwing a party. Unless you monitor everyone, dole out the refreshments to only those who are 21 or older and rule the party with an iron fist, someone under 21 may be having a drink on you. Providing alcohol to a minor is a Class A misdemeanor, even if the person throwing the party and providing the alcohol is also a minor. As for those 21 and over, generally speaking they are responsible for their own drinking and behavior, not you.

On rare occasions, some over-zealous prosecutors have been known to stretch cases of fatal accidents involving drunken drivers by charging those who either provided the alcohol or let them drive.

Whether or not a charge can be proven in a court of law, police officers routinely charge the regular party throwers to discourage their fun. Just because it is a shaky or weak case, it can result in a night in jail.

Furnishing alcohol to a minor

Scenario No. 1: Your girlfriend's little brother makes you a deal: His friends will give you the money plus $50 if you buy the beer for their party. When they are busted in their dorm room for being totally out of control, one of them lets it slip that you bought the beer. BANG.

Scenario No. 2: You are in the middle of your apartment that is packed to the gills with hot chicks, dancing the night away. Everyone is helping themselves to the keg on the back porch, when the cops show up, start writing tickets and arresting people for MIP and public intoxication. BANG, BANG.

Scenario No. 3: You are out on the town and meet a hot girl who is in the club without the "over 21 wristband." No worries, you buy the drinks and give them to her and her friends. When TABC wanders through the club, they see her and her friends drinking and ask who bought the drinks. One of her friends points you out. BANG, BANG, BANG.

In each scenario, you may be arrested for furnishing alcohol to a minor, otherwise known as "contributing to a minor." The exception to this law is that you can provide alcohol to your child as long as you are visibly present when the minor consumes the alcohol.

HAZING, HOAXES AND PRACTICAL JOKES

What is hazing? The short answer is almost everything that used to be fun. But seriously, this has become a problem on college campuses, mainly in the Greek community. But it is no longer limited to fraternities and sororities. Other campus organizations, clubs and sports teams have been sanctioned and prosecuted as well. What were once harmless rituals and rites of passages have evolved into acts of brutality. Because of this escalation, the criminal law has stepped in.

The long answer: Any intentional, knowing, or reckless act that endangers the safety or mental or physical health of a student for the purpose of pledging, being initiated into, affiliating with, holding office in or maintaining membership in an organization. Examples include:

- Physical brutality (whipping, beating, striking, branding, electronic shocking, placing of a harmful substance on the body, trading swats, fights, boxing matches).
- Physical activity (sleep deprivation, exercise, exposure to the elements, confinement in a small space, kidnapping, drops).
- Consumption of a food, liquid, alcoholic beverage, liquor, drug or other substance.
- Activity that intimidates or threatens the student with ostracism.
- Activity that subjects the student to extreme mental stress, shame, humiliation, degradation or discourages the student from entering or remaining registered in an educational institution, or that may reasonably be expected to cause a student to leave the organization or the institution rather than submit to the acts.
- Activity that induces, causes, or requires the student to perform a duty or task that involves a violation of law.

Anyone who knows about a planned act of hazing or one that happened in the past and fails to report it to the officials could face charges. The fact that the pledge consented is not a defense. Hazing is a Class B misdemeanor, Class A if it results in bodily injury and a felony if it results in death.

Hoaxes and practical jokes

Dorm life: Who hasn't played some type of practical joke on a roommate? It's more important to try to have some harmless fun, and not take this activity to the degree that someone might actually get hurt.

Joe is hanging in the dorm with his roommate when the most obnoxious and crude guy in the building comes home. After he's in his room, Joe jams a stack of pennies between the door and jamb. Now the guy can't open his door. Sounds like some good, old-fashion fun, but Joe forgets about the door and the guy misses a final exam the next morning or there is a fire in the dorm that night and he can't escape.

Forget about the possibly of being charged with unlawful restraint. The death will undoubtedly create some very unpleasant and unexpected legal problems. Granted this is an extreme scenario, but strange and unexpected things do happen.

Dry ice bomb: One afternoon Joe and some buddies are bored and try a little experiment in the dorm parking lot. Joe's geeky chemistry lab partner takes an empty two-liter Coke bottle, fills it a quarter-full with warm water then jams a chunk of dry ice in and caps it off. Joe and the guys stand back as the pressure builds and then, BANG, it explodes causing people to spill out of the dorms. Someone even calls the cops.

Someone may be taken into custody for Class A misdemeanor prohibited weapon charges, unless the cops have a sense of humor or Joe can convince them they were actually testing the laws of physics.

Whether the "dry ice bomb" qualifies as a prohibited weapon would be up to the cops and D.A. to decide. After 9-11, people are a little on edge, and something like that could cause some unrest.

Potato guns: These contraptions do not fit exactly into any illegal category, but it could be argued that they very well qualify as a firearm because they "expel a projectile through a barrel by using the energy generated by an explosion." And that is the basic definition of a firearm in Texas. Certainly, if these are used in a way that causes injury or serious bodily injury they could be deadly weapons under Texas law. Be careful these things can cause serious injury to those trying to build or use the home-made "tater cannons."

Fun with laser pointers: Schmedley has gotten his hands on a laser pointer, you know, one of those little pen-like pointers used for presentations. You might have seen them at the movies when some annoying butthead like Joe continually points it at the screen. It becomes somewhat of a joke with the guys to use it for pranks at lectures, graduation ceremonies and anywhere else they can annoy people.

One evening as they are on the way to a movie, Joe drives by a university police officer working traffic control when Schmedley, sitting in the back, points the laser at the officer. BANG, the car is stopped and someone is arrested or ticketed for a Class C misdemeanor, not to mention all the other things that go along with being stopped, like being questioned, IDs run through for warrants and the car searched. It is unlawful to point lasers at police, firemen, EMS works and other uniformed officers.

It's just a joke, man! Just like drugs, fake drugs can get you into hot water. Hoaxes, pranks and practical jokes are fun, but if you're not careful in their planning, they can get the authorities involved. What makes this illegal is not only the intent, but also the harm or alarm to those subjected to the joke. For example, Joe could face charges if the "hoax bomb" was intended to make someone believe it was actually a bomb or it was designed to cause alarm or reaction of a government official who deals with emergency situations.

Charges of illegal restraint might apply when when Joe "pennied" the guy's dorm room door shut. Think assault or criminal mischief if he douses the same guy with five gallons of pudding as he leaves for a date.

Public nudity for fun

Flashing, streaking and just taking a leak: Indecent exposure is committed when a person exposes himself with intent to arouse or gratify the sexual desire of someone and is reckless about whether someone else is present who would be offended or alarmed by the act. This is a Class B misdemeanor.

The classic situation happens with young women at Mardi Gras, or the predilection of many young men to bear "to moon," or the time-honored tradition of the "pressed ham" on the car window or even the dated 1970s act of streaking. Although not calculated to "gratify the sexual desire of anyone," these "crimes" are all regularly prosecuted in the courts throughout Texas. If not taken seriously and vigorously defended, the charges could have lifelong effects. (See *Sex Crimes and Sex Offender Registration* section for more details.)

Let's say Joe is walking down the street late one night when nature calls. He goes behind a Dumpster, hopefully out of view, unzips, and the exhilaration of relief pours over him. All of a sudden a police cruiser's spotlight illuminates the entire area as Joe's essential human act of urination takes center stage. BANG, Joe's probably under arrest for indecent exposure. Joe really hasn't learned his lesson and does exactly the same thing a year or two later. If he's convicted a second time, guess what he is? That's right, a sex offender. Now he has a "reportable conviction. (See *Sex Crimes and Sex Offender Registration* section for more details.)

GAMBLING

The friendly wager and fantasy football: Let's say you lay a 20-spot on the Giants giving 5½ with some guy in science lab. Gambling is generally considered an illegal activity, but gambling in and of itself is not illegal. What makes it illegal is when someone other than the people betting receives some of the money, or if it was in public and if the odds are not the same for everyone. Simply put, since the bet is only between you two it's not illegal. The same goes for the football squares and the March Madness brackets. Nobody is making money without taking the same risk as everyone else. This goes for your fantasy football league.

Bookies: The real area of illegal gambling that you may actually bump into is with a bookie. It is a Class A misdemeanor to operate or participate in the earnings of a gambling place, to engage in bookmaking, or to sell chances or promote a lottery (better known as "the numbers"), including communicating information about bets, betting odds, or changes in betting odds. Historically, college campuses always have had some entrepreneurs, mathematics students or computer geeks who establish their own bookmaking system. Years ago, the University of Texas was home to one of the largest student/campus betting syndicates ever, which was ultimately busted and its administrators prosecuted.

How bookies work: A bookmaker's posted odds are not intended to be predictions. The purpose of odds is to make sure the bookmaker gets enough action on both sides of a bet to make sure that he wins no matter what happens. If the betting public's opinion is not reasonably balanced, a disproportionate amount of money would be wagered on one side of a game, thus forcing the bookmaker to gamble and bookmakers are not in the business to actually gamble. Really? Absolutely not! The bookie's role, strictly speaking, is to act as a broker, much like a stockbroker. His job is to "hold the money" and to charge a fee for that service. This is called the "vig" or "juice." This is the fee that the bookie charges even if the bet ends up even. It is this particular transaction that makes gambling through the "bookie" illegal, because the bookie will make money whatever the outcome.

Bookies come in all shapes and sizes and can turn out to be some very unpleasant people, especially when you lose and owe them money. If you really have to have action on the game, I suggest opening an account online with any number of legitimate gambling sites or keep the stakes low and gamble among friends.

The weekly poker game: The weekly poker game at Joe's buddy's apartment or even the recently popular Texas Hold'em tournaments are not illegal unless the house takes a cut. Authorities have taken the position that such tournaments held in public places, such as bars and clubs, especially if they have licenses to sell alcohol, cannot be legally held. It seems that the "public" nature can be interpreted as the illegal element of this violation.

Card houses exsist for two main reasons: to provide professional card players a venue and access to novice players and their money, and to take your money for the privilege of throwing you to the wolves. The fairest and safest game, if there is one, is at a legitimate casino. Remember, if you sit down at the table and don't know who the sucker is, it's you.

Online gambling: Many in law enforcement consider online gambling a violation of Texas laws. While this requires some hyper-technical interpretation, it is not entirely incorrect. On the other hand, Texas laws do not address online gambling directly; they rely on decades-old terms and references that are not accurately applicable to today's technologies. Geographic locations of servers, the financial institutions and the nebulous complex networks required further complicate the issues and make concrete statements extremely tenuous. Modern derivations continue to evolve. Online poker, sports books and fantasy sports all continue to evolve and adapt depending on how the legal winds blow. These industries continue to prosper and grow, however, and people who patronize these sites have not been the targets of investigation or prosecution in Texas.

THE GREAT OUTDOORS

Camping and fires: Joe and his buddies head out for a weekend of camping, male bonding and drinking in the woods. They head to the state park, set up camp, crank the jam box and start downing the beers, while some gather wood for the raging fire that has been lit near the campsite.

Whether you're in a private camping area or one of the many Texas state parks, there are probably rules that you are going to have to follow. Joe's outdoor party is probably going to experience some problems from the park ranger, most notably the fire and regulations that protect the other campers in the park from noise disturbances.

It is an offense to cause a disturbance between 10 p.m. and 6 a.m.

Fires in state parks must be contained to grills, fireplaces or fire rings. Under dry conditions, county officials regularly issue fire bans. Look for signs or ask at the gate for specific campfire information. Some primitive sites have fire rings and some beach sites allow ground fires on sandy areas, if approved by the park manager, but firewood may not be gathered unless authorized by the park manager.

Hunting and fishing: First off, know the size, bag limits, and season and you'll be OK. You must carry a license and the applicable stamps or permits, as well as a driver's license or personal identification certificate. You can check out all the regulations at the Texas Department of Parks and Wildlife website at tpwd.state.tx.us or by calling 800-792-1112 or 512-389-4800.

It is against the law to hunt or fish on privately owned lands or waters without the permission of the owner or the owner's agent. (Check out the *Trespassing* section of Chapter 10.) Always retrieve all wounded game birds and animals, kill them immediately and count them against your legal bag limit. Careful, though, you can't pursue a wounded animal across someone else's property line without his consent. Always know where you are and be careful where you shoot because it is against the law to discharge a firearm on or across a public road.

Boats and jet skis: Jet skis are considered "personal water craft" and the laws apply to them as if they're boats.

Joe and the boys are headed to the lake with dad's ski boat for a day of fun in the sun. They load up the skis, wakeboards, ice down the beverages, and head to Lake Travis. They spend several hours skiing and drinking beer, catching some rays and having a great time. Even the girls they managed to get to come along are having fun. As they are tooling around, headed to Devil's Cove for a rest and some company, the water cops pull up and ask to inspect the boat, not to mention question the driver about his paperwork and his alcohol consumption. BANG, the boys are in trouble. The driver is 17, intoxicated and there are several violations on the boat, namely, not enough life jackets and too many people on the boat. Never exceed a boat's capacity. The capacity plate is usually near the operator's position or on the boat's transom.

The DWI laws are basically the same for boats as they are for other vehicles, so take a look at the *DWI* section in Chapter 6 for a full explanation. All marine safety enforcement officers, law enforcement and game wardens have the authority to enforce boating laws. The U.S. Coast Guard has enforcement authority on federally controlled waters.

You must have a Texas Certificate of Number (registration) and a validation decal to legally operate your boat on Texas' public waters. The only exceptions are for sailboats under 14 feet in length and non-motorized boats such as canoes, kayaks, rowboats and rubber rafts.

Anyone born on or after September 1, 1993, is required to take boater education if they are going to operate personal watercraft, a vessel over 15 horsepower, and a sailboat longer than 14 feet.

Summary of required equipment and rules:

- Coast-Guard approved flotation devices for each person on board; children under 13 must wear a lifejacket.
- A personal flotation device must be worn if riding a personal water craft, while skiing or being towed.
- At least one "throwable" floatation device must be on the boat.
- At least one fire extinguisher must be on the boat.
- A whistle or horn must be one the boat.
- Skiing is prohibited between 30 minutes after sunset and 30 minutes before sunrise. Personal water crafts are not allowed between sunset and sunrise.
- Red and green side lights must be visible from at least one mile. White light, masthead and stern lights must be visible from at least two miles on a dark clear night and must be at least one meter higher than the sidelights;
- Boats are required to display an all-round white light whenever they're moored or anchored from dock between sunset and sunrise.
- Personal water crafts must have a lanyard-type engine cutoff switch attached to the driver, his clothes or personal flotation device.

It is illegal to operate a personal water craft within 50 feet of another boat or PWC, a person, a stationary platform or a shoreline, except when maintaining headway speed. It is illegal to operate a PWC in a manner that requires the operator to swerve at the last possible moment to avoid collision, and a PWC should not jump the wake of another boat recklessly or unnecessarily close to that boat.

Rivers and lakes: The state of Texas owns the water in every lake and natural stream, as well as the fish that live there, but the public does not have the right to fish or boat in private lakes or streams. This gets really complicated, especially since Texas land titles originated with Spanish or Mexican land grants, which did not distinguish between public and private streams on the basis of navigability.

Basically, you may boat, canoe, tube, swim, float, walk, wade, picnic, fish (with a license) even camp in public water, but you must be confined to the waters of the lake or stream and the streambed. You do not have the right to cross private property to get to or from the public water. Portage is sometimes necessary to scout a dangerous condition or safe route or to avoid it altogether by walking around. Anytime you portage, you may be flirting with criminal trespass and the defense of necessity. Your best bet is to minimize your intrusion on anyone's land unless absolutely necessary for safety.

Even though some private land along the coast is covered intermittently or continuously by tide waters, the general rule is "if you can float it you can boat it." As for wade fisherman in these areas, it is unclear if they may be trespassing.

Lastly, it is now a crime to drive a motor vehicle in the bed of a navigable freshwater stream, unless approved by a local river access plan established by a city, county, or river authority. This does not apply to the Red and Canadian rivers.

CHAPTER 8
SELF-DEFENSE, GUNS, AND WEAPONS

CERTAINLY, YOU CAN DEFEND YOURSELF, your girlfriend, friend or stranger, as well as your car, home and other property as you see fit. But how and to what degree you do so lawfully is limited to the interpretation of the law and the facts in each situation. Texas has the reputation that our communities and juries allow a little more force than most. I will give it to you straight and simple so you can understand the basic laws. The most important distinction to understand is that between force and deadly force.

SELF-DEFENSE

Use of force

A person may use force, the threat of force or even actual confinement to protect himself, except in response to verbal provocation alone, to resist an arrest or search by a peace officer (even if it's unlawful), when the person consents to the exact force used or attempted by the other person, or when the person provokes the other person.

The incident: As Joe works his way through the crowd at the club, a guy bumps into him spilling beer down the front of his shirt. Joe says "excuse me," while the guy responds with "fuck you, dick breath." Joe rears back and whacks him in the head with his beer bottle. BANG, the bouncers grab Joe, drag him through the club and hand him straight to the cops standing at the front door. This asshole's bad manners do not justify Joe hitting him with his beer bottle. If he had made these comments while raising his hand to apparently hit Joe, then Joe could have had used force to get the first shot.

"Let's step outside": Instead of acting impulsively, Joe asks, "Outside to settle this?"

They both head outside. In this situation both may have consented to the force, but this is difficult to employ at trial or when the cops drag them both to jail for disturbing the peace or some other public order type of offense.

Say Joe rips off his shirt, showing off his underdeveloped physique and sending the guy back toward the club. But then Joe tackles him as he walks back. Joe will face assault charges and the cops will take him to jail, no matter what the asshole said inside the club.

The arrest: The use of force to resist an arrest or search is justified only if an officer uses or attempts to use greater force than necessary to make the arrest.

As the bouncers hand Joe over to the cops, as they try to handcuff him, he wriggles around and flails his arms, apparently unwilling to cooperate. In the mild melee outside, a cop falls and sprains his knee and Joe's hand flails and hits him in the eye. Both of these things cause the cop pain. BANG, an additional charge of resisting arrest (misdemeanor) or assault on a peace officer (felony) are added to the assault on the asshole inside.

Threats: A threat to cause death or serious bodily injury by showing a weapon is generally justified, as long as you're trying to get the person to stop.

Instead of Joe's response with the bottle to the asshole's head, Joe tells him, "Leave me alone or I'll fuck you up." This is probably OK so long as his intent is only to create apprehension to get him to leave Joe alone. If Joe's comments are not reasonable for the situation and the asshole's aggression, he may be subject to a Class C misdemeanor assault or a terroristic threat (Class B misdemeanor).

Deadly force

Self defense: A person is justified in using deadly force if he believes it is immediately necessary to protect himself against an attempted use of deadly force if a reasonable person in the same situation would have not retreated. The retreat requirement does not apply when someone has unlawfully entered your home. You can also use deadly force to prevent aggravated kidnapping, murder, rape or robbery.

The dark alley: You and Joe find yourselves outside the club after closing time and you both see the asshole and his buddies hanging around in the parking lot. As you walk toward your car, the asshole and his friends begin to walk in your direction. He has a baseball bat in his hand and his friends have circled around. There is nowhere to go, and even if there was, you feel they would follow you. As he continues toward him, Joe grabs an empty 40-ounce bottle and whacks the asshole in the head as he rushes toward him. You both run off. Unfortunately for the asshole, the bottle shattered and cut his jugular vein and he bled to death within minutes. Joe's actions appear reasonable under the circumstances and he will most likely avoid prosecution.

Defense of another person: You may use deadly force against an attacker to protect another person if you would be justified to use it to protect yourself and you reasonably believe that it is immediately necessary to protect the person from serious injury or death.

The good guy: As you and your buddies leave the bar at closing time, you see a struggle behind one of the cars. As you get closer, you hear a girl say "no." Her shirt is torn and some guy is holding her down against the trunk of a car. You are justified in using force against the guy to protect her from injury. If it is reasonable that you think he is trying to rape or seriously injure her, then your actions in whacking him with a 2-by-4 in the head is probably justified as well.

Protecting your property: A person may use deadly force to protect his property if he reasonably believes it is immediately necessary to prevent arson, burglary, robbery, or theft, or mischief during the nighttime, and he reasonably believes that the property cannot be protected any other way. This includes the use of deadly force to prevent someone from leaving after committing burglary, robbery, or theft during the nighttime, if he reasonably believes that the property cannot be recovered by any other way. (Nighttime is 30 minutes after sunset until 30 minutes before sunrise.)

The burglar: Late one night you are awakened by the sound of someone breaking into your apartment. You get out of bed and grab your gun. As you peer around the corner, you see some guy grabbing your TV. You shoot the guy and he drops dead in your living room. Traditional thinking is this is a "no-brainer." Even if you miss with the first shot and the burglar runs out the door with the TV, you are still justified in using your gun to try to stop him. The old adage that if you shoot 'em on the lawn, you better drag 'em in the house is not quite accurate. The critical factor is that the burglar is attempting to escape with the property; if you scare him off with the gunshot and he runs off without anything, don't shoot. It's probably not legally justified. A dead burglar on the lawn with a gunshot wound to the back will probably not escape serious scrutiny from the DA and a grand jury. That's not to say that it will get you indicted for murder, but Texas has seen its share of "frontier justice" excusing similar situations. That's where the drag 'em in off the lawn adage comes from, but I don't recommend it.

The pizza guy: Late one night you hear someone banging on your front door. You grab your gun and go to the door. You ask who is there and the response is, "Open the fucking door."

You ask again and the response is louder.

"You better open the fucking door."

"I've got a gun, get away from my door or I'll shoot."

"Fuck you."

You then fire a shot through the door and hear something that sounds like a person against the door. You open the door, and there's Joe, the pizza guy, with a gaping wound to the head. Joe had the wrong apartment and thought you were refusing to open and pay for the pizza. You have some serious problems and will probably have the case sent to a grand jury to review your actions. Your mistake does not excuse your actions. The circumstances, Joe the pizza guy's actions and your fear may affect how the matter is handled, but because of your actions, Joe the pizza guy is dead.

Use of device to protect property: Sometimes, people have rigged deadly weapons to kill or maim a person who enters a house or land. Dorm rooms are notorious playpens for practical jokes and sometimes people rig devices that will inflict injury or even death to anyone who may unknowingly enter.

If injury occurs in this sort of situation, the use of a device to protect land or tangible, movable property is only justified if the device is not designed to cause death and if the person who installed the device reasonably believes it to be reasonable.

To protect someone else's property: A person may use force or deadly force to protect the property of a third person if he reasonably believes that he would be justified in using similar force to protect his own property. This also applies if the person reasonably believes that the third person has requested his protection of property, or if he has a legal duty to protect the property or if the person whose property he is protecting is his spouse, parent or child.

The good guy is a hero: You and Joe walk out of class and into the parking lot. You see a guy approach a girl and pull out a gun. You run up from behind and hit him in the head with a metal stake, he falls and suffers a massive head wound. The school newspaper headline reads "STUDENT FOILS ROBBER." You become a campus hero and the girl you saved ultimately marries you after graduation. Although a bit risky, your quick action is heroic and legally justified under the circumstances.

The good guy is a chump: You and Joe walk out of the bar and see a man and a woman struggling next to a car. They are yelling and she repeatedly says "no," but the man grabs the keys, pushes her to the ground, jumps in and begins to start the car. Joe quickly runs over and pulls him out of the car as it begins to drive off. As the man falls from the car, his foot is crushed under the back wheel and the car runs into another vehicle in the parking lot. As the cops conduct interviews, it quickly becomes apparent that the guy was just trying to keep her from driving his car home drunk, their argument had gotten out of control, and he was just trying to go home. Since you both honestly thought you were trying to save her property, Joe will probably escape prosecution, but there's no guarantee. Although you can't always know what is going on, try to figure out what's happening before you take drastic action. But sometimes you have to rely on your instincts and act.

What is a reasonable belief? It is not necessary that there should be actual danger, as a person has the right to defend himself from apparent danger to the same extent as if it were real. Remember, the use of deadly force is OK when and to the degree you reasonably believe the force is immediately necessary. Also remember that a jury will decide what is reasonably necessary and to what degree.

What if someone else gets hurt? Even though a person is justified in threatening or using force or deadly force, if in doing so he recklessly injures or kills an innocent person, the justification or defense for his actions are unavailable in a prosecution for the reckless injury or killing of the innocent person. If you are trying to prevent someone from committing suicide or from hurting themselves to the point they would have serious bodily injury, then you can use force to the degree that you may reasonably believe the force is immediately necessary, but you may not use deadly force. If you are trying to save someone's life in an emergency then you can even use deadly force to the degree you reasonably believe is immediately necessary to preserve the life.

GUNS

Every citizen shall have the right to keep and bear arms in the lawful defense of himself or the State; but the Legislature shall have power, by law, to regulate the wearing of arms, with a view to prevent crime.

– Texas Constitution

Ownership of guns in Texas is about as "Wild West" as it gets in the United States. Ownership of handguns, shotguns, rifles and semi-automatic "assault weapons" are unrestricted and no state permit or license is required. However, ownership of a "machine gun" has federal law compliance issues. Handguns may be carried openly with a permit and concealed handguns are allowed on public college campuses.

Shotguns and rifles: Bubba can carry a loaded rifle or shotgun in his truck, whether it's in a rack or on the seat next to him. But unless he has a license, he can't have a handgun sitting on the seat, even if it's unloaded. Go figure.

Handguns: As of 2016, you can carry any handgun openly or concealed as long as you have a license The handgun must be carried in a shoulder or belt holster. Long arms do not require a license. If you're in your car and do not have a license, you will need to keep your handgun concealed.

If you are traveling to another state and you are spending at least one night away from home, you must carry the firearm and the ammunition secured in separate places and both outside of your reach. Under federal law, you should be OK, but federal law is vague about what constitutes traveling, so be sure you will be staying over at least one night and have checked the states' laws you will be traveling to and through.

Special care: A firearm must be stored in a place that cannot be accessed by a child under 17. It also must be secured with a trigger lock if there is reason to believe that a child may gain access to the firearm.

Not only can handguns cause you a problem if you don't carry them properly, you'll face legal problems if you sell, lease, loan, or give one to anyone you know intends to use it unlawfully. You also can't sell a handgun to someone who is intoxicated.

License to carry: A Texas License to Carry Handgun allows a person to openly carry a handgun and carry one in his vehicle. Contact Texas DPS or a certified instructor for class information and certification. The classes and certification are not difficult, but your attendance, attention and shooting proficiency will be required. Your criminal background will also affect your ability to obtain a license.

The privilege to carry a concealed handgun granted by this license may or may not be valid in other states, so check with the Texas Department of Public Safety regarding reciprocity agreements and those states' laws regarding your "carrying" in that state, even if just driving through.

Whether someone has a license to carry a handgun does not affect the right to use any firearm or other deadly weapon in defensive situations. This is completely dependent on the justification to do so under the laws relating to self-defense as explained earlier.

Places where you cannot carry your firearm (license or not):

Any property that has posted what is called a "30.06" sign. The requirements are precise and usually are not "legally" valid, but don't test these limits. Additionally, a firearm cannot be carried:

- By an intoxicated person.
- At an amusement park if a proper warning is given.
- In a place of religious worship if a proper warning is given.
- In a hospital or nursing home if a proper warning is given.
- At correctional facilities or within 1,000 feet of a correctional facility on a day that an execution is scheduled there if proper notice is posted.
- Court or offices used by a court unless pursuant to written regulations or written authorization from the court.
- At any polling place on Election Day.

- At any meeting of any governmental body if proper notice is posted.
- At sporting or interscholastic events, unless the license-holder is a participant in the event and a handgun is used in the event.
- At any racetrack.
- Inside schools or vehicles used by educational institutions.
- In establishments licensed to dispense alcoholic beverages for consumption on the premises, which derives 51 percent or more of its income from the sale of alcoholic beverages and has a conspicuous warning prohibiting firearms.
- Inside the secured area of any airport. However a person may carry any legal firearm into the terminal that is encased for shipment purposes and checked as baggage to be lawfully transported on an aircraft pursuant to airline and TSA regulations.
- Federal property, most of which will be marked with a sign that refers to Title 18 of the U.S. Code, usually the Post Office.

Campus carry

As of August 2016, LTC holders may carry handguns on all four-year state colleges and universities in Texas, but they must be concealed. In August 2017 this will also be applicable to all state two-year and junior colleges. Each campus administration may designate certain sensitive areas and buildings where concealed weapons will be prohibited. Such policies must be displayed on the official school website, as well as publicizing it among correspondence with the institution's faculty, staff, and students. Previous laws permitting the concealed carry with a license on open campus grounds and in locked vehicles in parking lots will remain unchanged.

The long and the short of it is that if you want to carry a handgun, get a license to do so, know the law and do so responsibly. If you hunt, shoot trap or sporting clays or just target shoot, know the rules and transport your weapons unloaded and in the right place. The quickest way to get an already nervous police officer more nervous is to produce a gun or have one where it's not supposed to be.

Other weapons: Handguns and rifles are not the only weapons that you cannot carry around. Certain knives, switchblades, knuckles (brass knuckles), clubs, explosive weapons, machine guns, short-barrel firearms, firearm silencers, armor-piercing ammunition, chemical dispensing devices and zip guns are also illegal.

Law enforcement officers and military personnel are exempted. Switchblades, spring-blade knives and short-barrel firearms are also exempted if they are antiques or curios.

CHAPTER 9
CARS, MOTORCYCLES, AND BIKES

CARS

PARKING, TOW TRUCKS AND THE BOOT: As is your usual custom, you pull into an open spot close to campus. You notice the parking meter, but as is your custom, you do not put any money in. After class, yet again, another parking ticket is on the window. You stuff it into the glove box.

One day after class you return to your parking space, but your car is gone.

"Holy shit, my car's been stolen," you exclaim.

But it is unlikely that your prized 1986 Buick has been lifted. You've been towed. You recall a similar situation last semester when you told your buddy Joe to just park close to the club and not to worry about the "NO PARKING" sign. Again, to your surprise the car was not there after a night of revelry.

In these cases, you have been lawfully towed. Some cities have instituted what is known as "the boot," a large steel cuff (usually painted bright yellow or red) that attaches to a vehicle's wheel and immobilizes it until you contact the city and pay up.

Police officers have the authority to tow a vehicle whose driver has been arrested, that has been in a collision and cannot be driven safely, or any other situation in which they reasonably feel necessary to remove the vehicle to clear traffic obstructions or if the vehicle is an instrument or evidence of a crime. Your car may be towed for numerous reasons from a private parking lot, such as obstructing a portion of a paved drive, abutting public road or marked fire lane. It can also be towed if it is preventing a vehicle from exiting a parking space in the facility or if it is parked in a space for disabled parking and does not have the required tag.

Private parking lots: Before you can be towed, you must have notice that parking is prohibited and may result in towing. Signs prohibiting unauthorized vehicles must be present at the time of towing and for the preceding 24 hours. Other proper notice is a conspicuous notice attached to a vehicle's front windshield outlining parking rules and listing a 24-hour telephone number to call if the vehicle is towed.

No parking signs: In order for a "NO PARKING" sign to be adequate, it must be conspicuously visible on the side of each driveway and entrance. If no definite entrances exist, signs must be permanently mounted at 25-foot intervals warning drivers that vehicles will be towed at owner's expense, the hours of towing enforcement, and a 24-hour telephone number to call if the vehicle is towed.

Apartment parking: Refer to the end of Chapter 10 dealing with apartment living. There are some different rules that cover apartment complex parking.

Towing and booting limitations: Parking facility owners are prohibited from receiving financial gain from a towing or boot company. They also may not have a monetary interest in a towing or booting company that removes unauthorized vehicles from their facilities.

Criminal violations are also included in these statutes and can result in prosecution for violations of many of the requirements under the statutes controlling this area.

Civil remedies allow for civil suits against a towing company, booting company, or parking facility owner who unlawfully tows or boots a vehicle. Civil judgements can result for damages arising from the removal, storage, or booting of the vehicle, as well as for towing, storage, or booting fees assessed in connection with the vehicle's removal, storage, or booting.

You are not required to prove negligence of a parking facility owner, towing or booting company to recover. If it has intentionally, knowingly or recklessly violated these provisions, it may be liable for up to $1,000 plus three times the amount of fees assessed in the vehicle's removal, towing, storage or booting. Seek the advice of an attorney if you wish to pursue civil remedies over and above the tow/boot hearing detailed below.

WTF is a boot? A "boot" is defined as a lockable road wheel clamp or similar device designed to immobilize a parked vehicle until it is unlocked or removed. You've seen 'em for years in cities that use them for deadbeat parking violators. A private parking facility owner may also clamp boots on unauthorized vehicles.

A boot operator must include a note stating:

- That damage may occur if the vehicle is moved.
- The date and time the boot was installed.
- The name, address, and telephone number of the booting company.
- A telephone number that is answered 24 hours a day to call for the removal of the boot.
- The amount of the fee for removal of the boot and associated parking fees.
- Notice of the right of a vehicle owner or operator to a hearing.

Once the boot is removed, the boot operator shall provide a receipt to the vehicle owner or operator.

The booting company must maintain a copy of the receipt for three years. A peace officer has the right to inspect and copy the records to determine compliance with the requirements of this section. Booting companies must also accept payment by an electronic check, debit card, or credit card for any fee or charge associated with the removal of a boot and cannot charge a fee for their use.

This racket is gaining traction in high density areas. Businesses with limited prime parking are hiring companies to monitor their lots and boot unauthorized vehicles.

So your car has been wrongfully towed or booted: There were no signs, or the meter was broken or your car was not abandoned ... you certainly have rights when it comes to a towed or booted vehicle.

If you think you were towed without probable cause, you can contest the tow through the court system at a special "tow hearing." Tow hearings are heard by a justice of the peace and are held more quickly and have lower filing fees than many other types of hearings.

Tow/boot hearing: To request a "tow hearing," you must deliver a written request to the justice of the peace within 14 business days after the car was booted or towed.

If you pay the booting or tow and storage fees before requesting a hearing, the company must give you written notice of your rights to a hearing. This notice should give you all the information you will need to draft the request for hearing, including where you should file it.

OK, you've done everything that's required for your day in court. What happens now? The court must hear your case within 21 days of your request. The burden is on you. Hearsay evidence (what other people said) is admissible, so long as the justice of the peace deems it credible.

If you request a tow/boot hearing, do your homework and be prepared with pictures or witnesses to support your position. Be respectful and dress appropriately. This will help in obtaining a favorable ruling.

So your car has been lawfully towed: First off, find out where your car is. Scrape up the money, get a ride to the storage lot and get it out as soon as you can. It can get really expensive to leave your car in the storage lot. Every day it's there, it racks up another day's storage fee on top of the original towing fee and there are other fees that are tacked on, such as a $10 preservation fee, which is charged if a tow truck or yard operator rolls up the window in the rain, as well as a call fee if the lot calls the owner to let him know that there vehicle is at the lot. Usually, city ordinances regulate how much an owner has to pay to get their car back, but I promise, it will not suit your budget to leave it in there until you think you can afford to get it out.

Damages from tow or storage: Now when you go to pick up that cherry ride of yours, remember to check it out before you sign a release. If there is damage consider making a note of it on any release required by the storage lot. Get a copy, with their signature on it, as well as request in writing the company's insurance provider and its policy number. You may consider filing a written claim with the tow truck company, storage facility or their insurance companies. Take some pictures of the damage while still at the storage lot.

There are statutory limitations on liability for parking facility owners. They are not liable for damages arising from the removal or storage of the vehicle if the vehicle was removed in compliance with the statutes.

The valet: After a great dinner with your new girlfriend, the valet wheels up in your vintage Yugo, but you immediately notice that the side mirror is ripped off and a nice scrape runs down the length of the car.

Valet parking services must have insurance for each employee who operates a motor vehicle. This must include liability, comprehensive, general liability, a garage insurance policy, a surety bond, or a deposit of $450,000. They must also display evidence of financial responsibility.

Back to your Yugo: Ask to see their insurance, get the policy number, the insurance carrier, the names of witnesses, the name of the owner, and take several pictures of the damage. Ask to talk to the owner if he is present, and try to iron it out immediately. Handle it just like a traffic accident.

Speeding tickets and other moving violations: One Friday after classes, the Aggie departs lovely College Station and speeds down the highway on his way to see his girlfriend at SMU in Dallas. He sets the cruise control on his pickup at 80 mph. The DPS Trooper sees him come over the hill and, BANG: the lights, the siren, the horror. The trooper saunters up to the window, and asks, "You got any ID?"

The Aggie responds, "About what?"

Everyone seems to push the envelope when traveling the highways. If you speed, be prepared to get tickets. Try to keep it within 10 mph of the limit and you will reduce your chances of getting pulled over. Always travel in the right lane, unless passing, because their radar guns are usually trained on the left or fast lane. If you are stopped, remember the helpful hints in Chapter 1 and politely sign the ticket. You are only acknowledging you got the ticket and you agree to appear in court. The ticket will contain information about the court and who to contact. Arguing with the officer or demanding to "see his radar" will not get you anywhere but maybe the local jail.

A speeding ticket is a Class C offense, which means that you cannot be put in jail if convicted. You can, however, be arrested for Class C offenses. If you refuse to sign the ticket, the police officer has no choice but to arrest you to make sure you appear in front of a judge. Your signature is simply your promise to appear in court on or before the date on the ticket.

Your options: When you receive a speeding ticket or other Class C ticket, there are four alternatives:

- Pay the ticket. The downside is that it will go on your record, possibly affecting your insurance rate. The upside is that it is over and done with.
- Ask to take Defensive Driving. The downside is that it will cost you a fee, you'll have to get your driving record; take the class (eight hours), and return the proof of attendance to the court. You can only take it once every year for a ticket. The upside is that it stays off your record and gives you a reduction in insurance rate.
- Set it for trial. Appear with or without an attorney, enter a plea of "not guilty" and ask for a jury trial. The court will give you a trial date or will notify you later. If you choose this route, the

downside is that you may want to hire an attorney. If trial day comes and the cop shows up, you will be expected to try the case in accordance with the rules of evidence and procedure, just like a lawyer. Sounds easy, but you are not familiar with the rules of evidence and questioning. There are plenty of lawyers who specialize in traffic tickets who are reasonable and worth the money. Ask around and you'll find the lawyers that specialize in this area. The upside is that your attorney will handle everything.

- If you have hired an attorney and have set it for trial and the cop showed up, the prosecutor may offer you deferred adjudication. This basically means that you will pay a reduced "administrative fee" and promise not to be convicted of a moving violation in certain period of time, usually 30 to 90 days. Once that period of time period has expired, then the case is dismissed. The downside is that you will pay the fee and have to watch yourself for the next month or so. If you don't, then it will be a conviction. The upside, it's dismissed.

Any effect on your driver's license is covered in the earlier section dealing with driver's license suspension issues and may arise if you continue to get tickets. (Read the sections dealing with *License Suspensions* in Chapter 3.)

The sweet looking sorority girl from TCU gets off work at the hospital and heads home to New Braunfels for Thanksgiving. As she crests the hill in the well-known speed trap, she sees the deputy sitting there with his radar gun; she looks down and realizes that she is going 2 mph over the limit. She immediately pulls over to the shoulder to wait for the cop. The cop comes to the window and asks for ID and insurance. As she gives it to the cop, he sees she is dressed in scrubs and asks if she's a doctor or nurse.

"No, a rectal extender," she replies

"Really?" the cop responds, "Never heard of one of those. What do you do exactly?"

"Well, whenever someone is gonna have a serious procedure, they are brought to me, where I stick my finger up their ass, then work my hand in and start stretching their rectum. I stretch and stretch and stretch until it is about six feet."

The cop is shocked. "What the hell do you do with a six-foot asshole?"

"Put him on the crest of a hill with a radar gun."

Driver's license points and surcharges: Texas has recently followed the lead of many other states in assigning "points" for various traffic offenses. DPS then charges a surcharge when the license is renewed. Anyone who accumulates six or more points during the preceding 36-month period is charged $100 for the first six points and $25 for each additional point. This applies whether the violation occurred in Texas or another state. DPS assigns two points for each conviction of a moving violation and three points for a moving violation that results in an accident.

You may ask, "What is a moving violation?"

Well, Grasshopper, I'll tell you: it's whatever the DPS decides, but basically it is speeding, failure to yield, running red lights and stop signs and those types of tickets. There are no points for speeding less than 10 percent faster than the posted speed limit and if it wasn't in a school zone. There won't be any points if court places you on deferred adjudication or allows defensive driving.

There is also a surcharge for certain other convictions, namely DWI or offenses relating to driving while intoxicated. DPS assesses a surcharge on the license of each person who during the preceding 36-month period has been convicted of any offense "relating to the operating of a motor vehicle while intoxicated." The surcharge for a first offense is $1,000 per year; $1,500 for a second or subsequent conviction within a 36-month period.

If there was a blood, breath or urine specimen that was 0.15 or above, then the surcharge is $2,000. (See *Should I Blow?* section of Chapter 7 for other reasons why you should or should not give a specimen if requested.) There are also surcharges of $100 for failure to maintain financial responsibility or if you are convicted of driving while your license is suspended or invalid.

Insurance: If you're going to drive, you need insurance for several good reasons. First, it's the law that you must have at least liability insurance, which protects others from damages to cars or property and injuries you may accidentally cause. Secondly, insurance can protect you from serious financial losses that can result from an accident.

What the heck Is SR-22? It is the form that insurance companies file with the DPS to verify and certify that you have insurance. The insurance company must notify DPS anytime the policy is canceled, terminated or lapses. "SR-22" insurance is not necessarily "high risk" insurance, but the insurance company will be quite curious as to why it is that you need it. You don't even have to own a car to get an SR-22.

So you've had an accident — what to do and not do: If you have an accident, under Texas law, it is necessary for you do a couple of things or you run the risk of being charged with a crime. What you must do and when you may leave the scene of an accident depends upon the nature of the accident. Most important, call for medical assistance if anyone is injured and provide basic first aid to anyone injured. Leaving the scene is not an option under the law.

You and our old friend Joe are driving home from the library late one evening and Joe swerves to miss a dog that runs into the road. As result of Joe's humanity, he accidentally side-swipes a parked car. No one is around. What should Joe do?

Under Texas law, an accident that results in damage requires the driver to stop at the scene or as close as possible and remain there until you have given your name, address, the vehicle's registration number and insurance information to the other drivers. You also must show your driver's license and provide reasonable assistance to anyone injured. Therefore, Joe must stop and locate the owner of the vehicle and provide his name and address if possible. If not, then he must leave a written note in a conspicuous place (usually under the window wiper or taped to the door window) that contains the driver's name and address and a statement of the circumstances of the collision. This also applies to situations where fixtures such as signs, light poles, fences, mailboxes or even landscaping is damaged from an accident. If this happens and you can't find the owner, make a report to local law enforcement within 10 days of the accident.

If you're involved in an accident and your vehicle can be safely moved, you should move it to a safe area or accident investigation site if available. It is not necessary to call the police, but if the accident resulted in death or injury and the vehicle is damaged to the extent that it cannot be safely driven, then you should immediately notify the authorities as soon as possible.

Anytime an officer arrives at the scene of an accident, it's a good idea to get the officer's full name and agency. Ask the officer when the accident report will be filed, its case number and how to get a copy.

Take careful notes of the date and time of the accident, the streets and city, the weather and road conditions, the direction and speed you and other drivers were going, and a brief description of how the accident occurred. Record the license plate, driver's license and insurance information numbers of each driver involved, as well as names, addresses and phone numbers of witnesses.

If no law enforcement officer comes to the scene and the accident resulted in death, injury or in excess of $1,000 then you must make a written report of the accident within ten days of the accident with local law enforcement.

CYA. Make sure you cover your own ass: Be careful if the other driver is hesitant to give you his insurance information or suggests suggests paying for the repairs himself. You can definitely agree to handle the repairs this way, but get his information just in case he has a change of heart.

Driver's license suspensions: Your Texas driver's license may be suspended or revoked for a lot of reasons. Alcohol-related suspensions make up the vast majority of situations as discussed in the *DWI* section in Chapter 7, but there are other reasons. Driver's license suspensions have become increasingly popular as a deterrent or, rather, punishment for other behavior, especially in drug cases and for outstanding warrants.

Because the Texas and U.S. Supreme Court have determined that driving is not a right, but a privilege, states can closely and increasingly regulate driver's licenses in almost any manner they see fit. Automatic driver's license suspensions occur upon a conviction. The length of the suspension depends on the type of conviction and the person's history. Below is a summary of automatic and other discretionary suspensions, but does not include every possibility.

Conviction of a crime: A person's license is automatically suspended upon final conviction for criminally negligent homicide (involving a vehicle); evading arrest or detention; DWI; intoxication assault; intoxication manslaughter; failure to stop and render aid (involving injury or death); possession/display or fictitious or altered driver's license; permitting another to possess yours; possessing multiple driver's licenses; fraudulently attempting to obtain a fictitious driver's license; any felony traffic code offense; any drug offense; and driving while license is suspended, revoked, or canceled. The Texas license is also subject to suspension for your actions in another state.

If your license is from another state and has been suspended, you are not eligible for a license in Texas.

Habitual violators — too many speeding and traffic tickets: A person who receives four or more moving violations in 12 months or seven or more moving violations in 24 months is subject to having his license suspended, as is anyone convicted of two or more violations of a driver's license restriction/endorsement, such as driving without "corrective lens" or outside of certain hours.

Insurance problems and accidents: If you are convicted of a second offense for no-liability insurance, your license is subject to a suspension until you file and maintain proof of financial responsibility (i.e. SR-22). If DPS receives notice that a person has canceled his insurance while the required to maintain an SR-22 is still in effect, suspension will re-occur.

If DPS receives notice that a person has been involved in an accident that occurred on a public street or highway that resulted in injury, death or property damages of at least $1,000, the uninsured driver who caused the damage is subject to license suspension. In order to get this type of suspension lifted, you must provide evidence of liability insurance at the time of the accident, pay for the damages and secure a full and final liability release, file an executed installment agreement or file a security deposit with the state along with an SR-22.

If there are no civil suits pending or unpaid judgments two years after the date of the accident, you can get your license reinstated. If there is an unsatisfied judgment arising out of a traffic accident that occurred on a public street or highway, the driver's license of the person who the judgment is rendered against is subject to suspension.

Delinquent child support payments: The Texas Attorney General's office is authorized to obtain an order for DPS to suspend and revoke a person's driver license for delinquent child support payments. The license will be revoked until the Attorney General's office or a court orders DPS to reinstate the license.

Medical reasons: The Texas Department of Health Medical Advisory Board is a panel of physicians that reviews the medical condition of a person to make sure he can safely operate a car. It may investigate when someone applies for or renews his driver's license and he provides medical information that calls into question his ability to safely operate a motor vehicle. It might also become involved when DPS is notified by a family member, a physician or a citizen about a license-holder who they think has some medical condition that prevents them from safely driving.

If the panel determines a person cannot safely drive because of his medical condition, DPS will revoke his driver's license.

Reinstatement: Once the suspension period is over, you must file for reinstatement of your license with the Department of Public Safety. Adults convicted of a drug offense are required to complete a drug education program. Minors also have some educational requirements. A certificate of completion must be forwarded to DPS. If you have any questions about what you must do to for reinstatement, call DPS-Driver Improvement and Control at 512-424-2600. DPS may also require the filing of an SR-22 as a pre-requisite to a license suspension being lifted. (See the above-section about insurance for a more detailed explanation of SR-22.)

Clearing up out-of-state problems: In order to lift or prevent the suspension of a Texas license because of another state's notification, you will have to obtain a clear status from that state's licensing agency. Upon confirmation of the clear status from the out-of-state licensing agency, contact the Department of Public Safety at 512-424-2600 for the clearance/compliance to be applied to the Texas driver record. For this type of cancellation, documents submitted to DPS from an out-of-state court are not acceptable as proof of compliance. Compliance must originate from that state's driver licensing agency. DPS may also revoke a driver's license if the person has not complied with the terms of a traffic citation received in another state.

MOTORCYCLES

For the purposes of this section, "motorcycles" are also motor-driven cycles and mopeds.

These require a specific Class M driver's license, which may be issued to a 15-year-old that restricts the rider to a moped or a motorcycle with a piston displacement under 250cc (the restriction may be removed upon the person's 16th birthday). A road test is required for the Class M license, but not for a moped license.

The traffic laws are the same for motorcycles as they are for other vehicles, with the exception of some equipment requirements. Otherwise, know the traffic laws and follow them just like driving a car. One exception is that single rider motorcycles are allowed to drive in lanes designated for multiple passengers such as bus, carpool and high-occupancy lanes.

The helmet law: Anyone who operates or rides a motorcycle on a public street or highway must wear approved protective headgear. Any peace officer may stop and detain a person who is riding a motorcycle to inspect the person's protective headgear for compliance with safety standards.

Exception: A person 21 or older may be exempt from wearing a motorcycle helmet if he has completed an approved motorcycle operator training course or is covered by a health insurance plan providing at least $10,000 in medical benefits for injuries incurred as a result of a motorcycle accident.

Organ donors: An old joke around emergency rooms is that anyone on a motorcycle without a helmet is just an organ donor. That being said, I guess this is as good a place to talk about it as anywhere. It is also known as a "Statement of Gift" and anyone who wants to be an eye, tissue, or organ donor may execute a statement of gift by signing and carrying a donor card.

A statement of gift on your driver's license no longer has force and effect. There are a few things you need to do to be an organ donor.

Make sure your family knows about your decision to donate, sign a Uniform Donor Card, and have two family members sign the card as witnesses, and carry the card in your wallet at all times. If you haven't told your family you're an organ and tissue donor – you're not! If you're in an accident and die, the doctors and hospital personnel will ask your family members for their consent to donate your organs and tissues. Knowing your wishes will help your family make this decision easier for them.

BICYCLES

Texas defines a “bicycle” as a device that a person may ride and that is propelled by human power and has two tandem wheels, at least one of which is more than 14 inches in diameter. This typically includes a moped. The traffic laws apply to bicycles, which means that a bicyclist must abide by the rules of the road, just as if he were driving a car. The flip side is that a bicycle has as much right to the road as a car. One common myth is that you can be arrested for DWI on a bike. NOT TRUE. DWIs only apply to motor vehicles. If intoxicated and riding a bike, there are other offenses that may be breached, such as public intoxication and various “dangerous” traffic laws.

Other legal guidelines that will keep you out of trouble:

- Only ride a bike on or astride a permanent and regular seat attached to the bicycle.
- Don’t “pump” or try to carry more people that the bike is designed to carry.
- Don’t carry an anything that prevents you from using at least one hand on the handlebars.
- Don’t “hitch a ride” from other vehicles on the road.
- Nighttime presents additional requirements:
- A lamp on the front of the bicycle that emits a white light visible from a distance of at least 500 feet in front of the bicycle.
- A red reflector on the rear that is visible from 50 to 300 feet or a lamp that emits a red light visible from 500 feet.

Parking bikes: You can park your bike on a sidewalk so long as it doesn’t impede the normal and reasonable movement of pedestrian or other traffic on the sidewalk, but double-check with campus parking, as more stringent rules may apply on campus.

CHAPTER 10
APARTMENTS, LEASES, ETC. FINDING YOUR NEW PAD

YOU HAVE SERVED YOUR TIME in the dorms and are able to look for off-campus housing. Maybe it'll be an apartment by yourself or an old house with five others. Maybe your dorm has been overrun with rats or your roommate has dropped out of school and you have two weeks to find a new place to live. One option is your car or a friend's couch for the rest of the semester or a quick decision and sign a lease. In any event, after an extensive search online or even driving around looking for the "for lease" signs (my recommendation — usually a better deal and better landlords), you find the right place.

Someone else is looking also and the person showing you the property tells you it will go fast. You're anxious to sign the lease as soon as it is placed in front of you. Hold on a second and resist the urge. What makes you think that your best interests as a tenant will be protected? You are responsible for your decisions now, so look out for yourself. Your desire to find a place after long hours searching can push you into signing on the dotted line. Before you sign, take your time and make sure you've read and understand all of the language in the lease, including the fine print.

The lease

A couple of terms you should know:

Lessee: The tenant (person renting the property).

Lessor: The landlord (person who owns or manages the property).

Lease: The actual written document that is the lease contract.

There are many more purposes for a lease other than your agreement to pay your rent each month and keep your apartment in good condition. Most important are the responsibilities of your landlord, which should be clearly outlined in this contract, so it's obviously in your best interest to read the lease carefully. If you're ignorant of the lease terms, you could find yourself blindsided several months later when your landlord holds you responsible for damage or some other breach of the lease and subsequently asks you to move out. What if you've got to move before your lease expires? The lease will outline your financial obligations should you need to back out for any reason.

Some leasing offices and landlords will place a lengthy, "standard" lease in front of you and downplay or simplify its terms. They're probably not trying to trick you, but are more likely in a hurry. Don't let their schedule dictate your decision and don't ever feel pressured or hurried. Instead, move off to the side, allow the leasing agent or landlord to accommodate other potential tenants and take your time to read the lease until you understand all of its terms. Make sure to take time to look for the sections dealing with late payment of rent penalties, security deposits, maintenance responsibilities and any prohibited activity. Even if you've read and signed a lease before, don't think they're all the same. They're not. Once you sign the lease and give a deposit, you're usually locked into its terms or at least will forfeit the deposit if you don't move in. Find out before signing what the consequences will be if you change your mind before moving day.

You may not realize that under the law you're entitled to request changes to the lease before signing it. In fact, you can request any modification you want so don't be afraid or intimidated from asking for changes. Remember, the person you are dealing with may be the same person you have to deal with when you want something fixed or your deposit returned, so be reasonable and respectful during the initial negotiations. If the landlord agrees to your terms, make sure the new terms are written on the lease itself (in ink, not pencil), dated with both party's initials next to them. Make sure you are given a copy of the executed lease before you leave and always keep a copy. Spoken promises will never hold up in the event that you have a disagreement over lease terms with your landlord.

Let's say you've agreed to lease the property, but only if they replace the carpet, fix the leaking toilet and allow your Labrador Retriever to live with you. Get it in writing with the date and a signature. If the landlord refuses to put any of the agreements in writing or suddenly makes some excuse why they shouldn't be included, warning bells should go off. No matter how cool the pad is, a bad landlord can make any place a miserable place to live. Move on and keep looking for the right place.

What if it's too late? You signed the lease and moved in without getting the new agreements in writing and now you keep requesting that those agreements be satisfied, like maintenance or repairs that have never been done. Threatening to withhold payment of your rent isn't a good idea. If there were a court battle, there's a good chance your landlord will win if you withhold rent payments without a signed agreement detailing your right to do so. Not only could you be facing stiff monetary penalties, you could find yourself evicted and looking for another place to live. The State Bar of Texas suggests that tenants who withhold rent can face penalties of up to three times the amount of rent they withheld.

There are really only three situations where a tenant can withhold rent:

- If the tenant first received a court order allowing him to withhold rent if the landlord didn't perform agreed-upon repairs or meet various conditions.
- If the tenant made repairs in his or her own unit and paid for them out of pocket; if the landlord was aware of and approved those repairs and the lease clearly stated that deductions in rent could be made under those circumstances.
- If the tenant has terminated the lease because the landlord

or apartment management company broke the terms of the written lease agreement with respect to his responsibility for repairs, or if the utilities have been cut off unlawfully.

Usually, those who have rental property, especially in college towns, are not there to take advantage of the students. The owners have likely made a handsome profit from their investment property but they are also interested in preserving their property in good order to continue to keep the property profitable. The bottom line is that you should always look out for yourself when entering into any kind of contract or lease.

Moving in: Now you've done your homework, found the right place, read the fine print, understand all the terms, signed the lease and even paid the deposit. One last thing before you move in: Inspect the property thoroughly. Make notes of all defects, no matter how small. If there is rust in the sink, write it down. Small nail holes in the wall? Write it down. If the door doesn't shut properly, write it down. If the toilet flushes funny, make a note. Take pictures of these conditions if possible, and make the landlord sign off and date all of your notations. Give him a copy and keep the original. This will come in handy down the road when you move out if a dispute arises over the return of your deposit.

Repairs: Ideally, your landlord is easily accessible for repairs or other issues and takes care of his business. However, if he doesn't and you need a repair, make your requests in writing, sent through the mail with a return receipt requested (it costs a little more than just the stamp). Documentation is essential. Keep your lease and paperwork or receipts relating to the property. Don't rely on a phone call, it doesn't prove a thing. Put it in writing!

Outside of some minor ones that are your responsibility, the landlord or management must make repairs within a reasonable time to correct conditions that threaten your health or safety. This can be anything from plumbing and electrical problems to common areas of the property in some instances. Look over your lease to see if it details your responsibilities for repairs. If not, then it falls upon the landlord to keep the property in proper repair.

The last resort is to make repairs yourself. After you have made the requests, put the landlord on notice and no repairs have been made within a reasonable time, you may make the repairs yourself and deduct that amount from the next month's rent. This, however, is a last resort and one that may have some risks involved. Double-check your lease and be sure that you have given the landlord all opportunity to make the repairs before resorting to making the repairs yourself.

The landlord or management cannot retaliate against tenants who ask for repairs. An eviction, rent increase or other adverse action within six months of a request for repairs is presumed to be retaliatory unless the landlord can show a valid reason for his actions.

The "month to month" lease: Let's say you've lived in the house or apartment and your lease date is almost up but you want to stay longer. If you pay the rent after the lease date expires, and the check is cashed, then the lease automatically becomes a "month to month" lease. This means that as long as you pay the rent on time and the landlord cashes the checks without giving some form of notice, this arrangement continues until one of the parties makes a change.

Lease termination — splitting or thrown out? Your lease is almost up and you want to move or the landlord wants you out. The party that wants to terminate the lease must give notice before the rent due date or lease termination date, usually the same. The amount of notice required is usually in the lease and it is usually 30 days. If they don't give at least 30 days' notice, then the notice rolls over to the next rent due date. For example, let's say the lease ends on January 31 and the rent is due on the first day of the month. You got notice on January 3 from the landlord that she is terminating the lease and is requesting you vacate the property by February 1. You actually have until March 1, because you are entitled to at least 30 days' notice in our example or however many days the lease dictates.

Lock out and eviction: One afternoon, you are be-bopping back to the pad for your afternoon nap. You get to the door and your key doesn't work; you realize that the landlord has locked you out and, more important, locked your stuff inside.

You think back to the last time you paid rent and about all those late notices the landlord kept sending you. Generally speaking, the landlord does not have the right to lock you out for failing to pay the rent. Before locking you out, your landlord must tell you when the locks will be changed and where you can get new keys without having to pay any of the owed rent.

The landlord must go through eviction proceedings to forcibly remove someone from the home. The eviction process usually takes several months and requires an order signed by a judge. If you find yourself in this situation or are served with legal papers, usually a suit for forcible entry and detainer, immediately contact an attorney or seek legal advice through your school's student services.

Security deposit: The end of the semester is coming up and you plan to backpack through Europe for the first half of the summer and follow Widespread Panic for the other half. So you are going to put your futon, milk crates and cinder blocks in storage for the summer. You have given the proper amount of notice that you are terminating the lease and moving out.

Remember that security deposit you put up before moving in and are planning to have in hand for your travels? Good news, you are entitled to get that back so long as the property has not suffered from you living there. You have some responsibilities if you want to get your deposit money back. Vacating the property clean and without any unusual damage will usually do the trick, but taking the time and making the effort to make small repairs, such as nail holes in the walls, will help. Lastly, remove everything, including all trash, and clean the whole apartment. Landlords commonly keep a portion, if not all, of the deposit for cleaning.

When you are ready to turn over the keys, get your list of

defects that you made when you moved in and go through the property with the landlord to compare. Take pictures of the condition of the property when you left it.

Landlords are not entitled to keep your deposit without a valid reason. The lease should give you a good idea of what is expected of you upon vacating the property. If you have been out for over 30 days, send the landlord a return-receipt letter demanding the deposit or an itemized accounting and reasons for its retention. When you get the landlord's response, compare her complaints with your list of defects that you made when you moved in. This will help if you have to fight the landlord for the return of the deposit. If she has good reason for using the deposit to make repairs (such as the hole in the carpet from your dog's incessant digging and chewing or the huge red punch stain left from that birthday party you had for 300 of your closest friends), then you may consider writing it off. But if you have taken care of the place, cleaned it before you left and didn't destroy anything, you should get most, if not all, of your deposit back.

Remember, you are not entitled to skip that last month's rent payment, thinking the security deposit will cover it, unless the lease specifically states that this is an option.

The real key to enjoying where you live is your relationship with the landlord or manager. Keep it friendly but business-like and you will have a much better chance at getting the repairs you need taken care of, avoiding any unpleasant confrontations and eventually getting your deposit back in full.

Moving? Don't forget to forward your address: Since you are probably a student, you are going to move a lot. Remember to fill out a change of address form at the Post Office or online so your mail will be forwarded to you new address. Also change the address on your driver's license. The most important reason for doing it is if a bill hasn't been paid or if you forgot about a ticket and it has gone to warrant. If these go into the "undeliverable" bin, then you'll never know about it and it will eventually come back to haunt you when you least expect it.

Living with roommates: You have found the best place to live, but you need some roommates to help out with the rent and bills. No problem, your best friend needs a place too, and what fun you'll have sharing a place. Conflicts can arise between even old friends who now are living together. Things like that annoying habit your roommate has of leaving the dishes in the sink for a month or playing the stereo at full force at 4 a.m. the night before your mid-terms. There is no magical advice that will help with personality conflicts, just some helpful advice from someone who has been there:

- Know who it is that you are planning to live with, his habits and living needs, and even his girlfriend. You may find that you spend almost as much time with her as the roommate.
- Be tolerant of those annoying habits and needs.
- Be considerate, remembering that you probably have annoying habits.
- Address problems as they arise, without letting them multiply, ultimately resulting in a confrontation.
- Remember that you were friends before living together, so you must be able to get along. Try to do so now as roommates. Go out have a beer and talk it out as friends.
- Establish some basic responsibilities that each has for the common good of the house (i.e. bills, cleaning, etc.), but remember don't go overboard with the rules.
- Be flexible.

Multiple roomates and the lease: If you sign a lease and your roommates don't, then you will be held responsible for whatever damage they cause and will be solely responsible for the rent. Most properties will require everyone living there to be on the lease. However, this is not always a disadvantage. If you are the only person on the lease, then you can control who lives there, but make sure to check the lease provisions regarding the number of people allowed to reside on the premises. If you chose to do this, remember, you have now technically become a sub-lessor and are subject to the same constraints as the lessor or landlord to your tenants.

The amenities of modern life (electric, cable TV, Internet and utilities): Now that you have a place, you'll need utilities, Internet and maybe even cable or satellite TV. These services sometimes require a deposit. You might be able to avoid a deposit with a co-signer who agrees to be responsible for the bill if you don't pay it.

It is important to take these accounts seriously. For most students, these accounts can be the first steps in establishing positive credit ratings. So if they are reported as default accounts that go uncollected, collection agencies will hound you for years. Your credit will suffer, affecting your ability to buy a car or house for years. Most people, especially students, don't realize this until it is too late. Take the responsibility to pay these accounts as they come due and this basic cornerstone establishing a positive credit report will be well worth the effort later in life.

Trespassing: A person commits trespassing if she enters or remains on property without consent or if she fails to leave the property after receiving notice that her entry is forbidden.

Trespassing is generally a Class B misdemeanor. But it's a Class C misdemeanor if it is on agricultural land and a Class A misdemeanor if the trespasser is carrying a deadly weapon.

The most important thing to remember from this section is that if someone is on your property or in your house that you do not want there, simply inform them that they are no longer welcome and ask that they leave. If they refuse and stay or leave and enter again, this will allow you to call the police to have them arrested for trespassing. You must allow them a reasonable opportunity to leave before the police will do anything, but it may become necessary to either prevent someone from entering your property or ejecting someone who has worn out his welcome.

If you are asked to leave someone's house or property, including a club/bar/party and you remain, you could be arrested for trespassing. This exclusion can even extend into the future without end.

For example, you and Joe are at the icehouse having some

pops with your pals. After some hours of merriment, your group decides it would be great fun to hold a fencing tournament on top of several pool tables, implementing the pool cues as foils. The manager approaches and informs you that you all are no longer welcome and to never come back. If you refuse to leave, the manager is well within his rights to forcibly remove you or call the cops to arrest you for trespassing. Months later, you forget about the ugly display of drunkenness, not to mention the terribly bad form displayed during your fencing match, and return with your girlfriend. But the manager recognizes you. Again, he is well within his rights to forcibly remove you or call the cops to arrest you.

By the way, firefighters and emergency services personnel are excluded from the trespass statute as long as they are responding to an emergency.

Parking: Certainly, you can see the situation where a landlord may want to tow your car out of the apartment parking lot. Granted, it leaks oil as fast as you can fill it and the tires always lose their air in three days, but there are some rules that apply before it can be towed. And there are some that you must follow as well.

You are not allowed to park in a restricted parking space, in a tow-away zone, in front of a gate or a garbage collection area. And, in a killer for college students, you may not park a vehicle that is leaking hazardous fluid. Semi-trucks are not allowed either.

The following are commonly used by property management, but are not valid. The landlord cannot tow your car merely because the vehicle does not display registration or license plate. A contract provision providing for the removal for these reasons is valid only if the provision requires the owner or operator of the vehicle to be given at least 10 days written notice that the vehicle will be towed if it is not removed.

CHAPTER 11 CREDIT CARDS

CREDIT CARDS AND THE DARK TRUTH

Whether or not your realize it, you are probably seeing a lot credit-card marketing. As a matter of fact, you have probably just bought this book at the friendly campus bookstore, which not only overcharged you for this semester's books, supplies and sweatshirt, but has also shoved credit-card offers down your throat by placing flyers in your bags. Just as weird are the credit- card marketing firms hanging out on campus, at sporting events, and at spring break, giving away T-shirts, videos, beer mugs, and more. Think about it, a free T-shirt just to sign up? Why?

You are a prime target for the corporate consumer-based society engrossed with capitalism (the making of money) and consumerism (the spending of money). You are the soon-to-be educated, upper-middle class that consumes a vast majority of the world's resources, which is exactly why the credit industry will want your business. In order to set their hooks in you early, the marketing companies want you to sign and spend, notwithstanding the reasonable reality that a person should have an income that at least exceeds their spending to rationalize the need for a credit card.

The extreme advantage these corporations have is that most of you have not been educated on the harsh reality of credit. A recent Fannie Mae Foundation report stated that 78 percent of college students have a credit card, an 11 percent increase from 1998. The same report showed that the average college student is about $3,000 in debt, not including their student loans.

The banks and credit card companies don't even care if you max out your cards. Hell, they want you to do it. Why? Because they know what happens when you max out your card and you are desperate.

Hello Mom and Dad? Can you send me some money?

Or you get a good job and ultimately pay down the debt after they have been sucking the interest out of you for years. They also know that most people keep their first credit card for an unbelievably long period of time and they also know when you get out of college and start making good money, you'll one day use it to buy a TV, a computer, cell phones, travel or maybe even a down payment on a Mercedes.

College students graduate with degrees in business and finance year after year, ironically with a large chunk of credit-card debt. These former students will probably struggle for years to pay off the debt or repair their credit at a time when they really need good credit to get their lives going, like buying a car, a house and the other things that come up in the years following college. Granted, you are not worried about those things now, but believe me, your credit, especially bad credit, will follow you around like an annoying little brother for a long time and, worse, will keep you from enjoying the life you have spent many years trying to achieve.

One day, in desperate need for a clean T-shirt, our old friend Joe finds himself walking through the quad one winter day when he stops to fill out the painless and harmless application. Walking from the table with a clean shirt in his backpack, he thinks nothing of it and goes about his business. A couple of weeks later, guess what appears in Joe's dorm mailbox? A shiny plastic card with a modest credit limit.

Spring break is bearing down and Joe's bank account has all

but vanished. Then the words that you heard from the marketing rep at the table weeks ago come to mind: "You'll need a credit card for travel, where are you going on spring break this year? Padre Island, skiing in Aspen?"

Now Joe actually can go. His brain practically makes him think that someone else is paying for the trip. Joe tells himself, just the essentials: hotel, food, and partying.

Spring break was great. Joe was true to himself. He thought he only charged the essentials. But when the bill comes in, he is reminded about the bar tab from the night he met that girl and her friends, not to mention the new surfboard and the small cash advance he needed to fund the last night's after-hours party in the condo. Let's say Joe only spent $500 on spring break, but to make it through the rest of the semester, Joe has to stop at the ATM for cash advances on his credit card because his checking account is low. He even puts some beer, gas and food on it.

Even if Joe's credit card has 9 percent APR, many credit cards charge a much larger APR, like 19.3 percent on cash advances. Many also have a 2 percent fee on top of the amount you withdraw.

Let's see how it's working out for Joe as he ambles along paying the minimum payment. The next year, while he's paying four times what he should for his books, the friendly campus bookstore slips another credit card application in his bag. Wow, another card. Let's apply, because the other one's filled up from spring break, cash advances, clothes, whatever.

Joe's graduating next May and he'll get a good job, and BANG, pay off the credit cards easily. Joe is starting to learn the intricacies of personal finance and how to make money magically appear where there is none. Every now and then Joe bounces a few checks to the credit card company, because he was playing the float game. Now Joe's bank and the credit-card company slap him with $30 fees. These fees are adding up to more than the entire monthly minimum payment. Joe is paying more $100 a month in late fees and does not even notice that it's piling up.

Minimum monthly payments don't keep up with the late fees. And, by the way, the bounced checks end up on your credit report, which we will talk about a little later. Remember the annoying little brother? He may prevent you from opening a checking account in the future or get the new car you were hoping to reward yourself with after graduation.

At this point you're saying, This guy's crazy, he has no idea who I am. Joe's an idiot. Even smart people can caught up in this mess. It's called deficit spending. Think about it, this is the same spending philosophy that the U.S. government practices. This is exactly the pattern that college students fall in to every year, with many owing $3,000 to $8,000 when they graduate.

"The dark truth be damned, I need a credit card." OK, so you still need or want a credit card. Be smart and follow the advice above and you should be O.K., but one credit card is enough for a college student. If you think you need another credit card, it's the first red flag that you have a credit problem. Do you think any of the aggressive marketers on campus will tell you that?

Stick with an "unsecured" card from a reputable bank without an "annual fee" and shop for a low interest rate.

Stay away from "secured" credit cards. Many are scams, or have such ridiculous conditions that it should alert you to stay away. Many require that you have money in the bank to cover them or can only be used to buy their overpriced, crappy products from their catalogue. If your credit is really that bad you should reconsider getting yet another card and more debt. Go cold turkey until you get your debt under control.

You should also seriously consider staying away from any department store card even when it is luring you with an offer to give you 10 percent off today's purchase. They don't to tell you that the APR on department store credit cards is usually around 20 percent, and that most people don't bother to notice that it's much higher than their MasterCard or VISA.

Tricks to avoid credit card fees: One month something happened and you were a little late paying your bill. BANG, there appears the dreaded late fee. Call up your credit card company and ask it to remove the late fee. If it's your first time, you'll likely get a 10-second lecture about the importance of sending your payment seven days in advance to allow for snail mail. If they don't give in, threaten to close your account and transfer your balance to another card. They make money when you have accounts with balances each month. The last thing they will want to do is lose you if you normally pay on time. Same goes for the annual fees. Call up the credit card company and tell them that you have many other cards that don't charge annual fees. Tell them that unless they remove the annual fee you will cancel your account or transfer the balance to another card. If they really want your business, they'll cave. If not, be ready to cancel the account. You should never have to pay an annual fee. You pay enough in interest, but if you have credit problems or a history of late payments, you may not have a chance with this one. It's still worth a try.

I have someone else's credit card: If you found it, call the credit card company or bank immediately. They will likely advise you to destroy it or send it to them. If someone gave you a card with express authorization to make a transaction, only make the transaction authorized. If you are tempted to make a charge or two without proper authorization, DON'T. Abuse of a credit or debit card – better known as fraud – is a state jail felony for each transaction. More serious offenses may be charged if the transactions are approved and property is transferred.

CHAPTER 12
SPRING BREAK

DON'T GET BURNED: I don't mean sunburn. If it's wintertime, that age-old rite of passage is just around the corner. I'm talkin' about spring break: The annual migration to Daytona Beach, South Padre Island, Steamboat Springs, Mexico, Mardis Gras. Besides attracting thousands of students, these hot spots also attract those looking to make a buck.

Each year, hundreds of college students get ripped off by fraudulent spring break offers that promise — but fail to deliver — that much-needed "fun in the sun." Travel fraud is a growing problem and college students seem to be attractive targets for dishonest travel operators. Don't be one of those who get taken. Not all fraudulent offers involve losing money. Some are simply misleading. The lodging may not be what you expected or the package might not include flights or confirmed hotel space. Also watch out for additional fees.

If you plan to crash in your car or on someone's floor and bathe in the ocean or gas station restrooms, disregard this section. Otherwise, make your spring break vacation plans early. Here are a few suggestions:

- Be wary of offers that promise "the moon" for a very low price, or require immediate purchase to lock in the announced rate.
- Before paying anything, request all details of the trip in writing, including total cost, restrictions, cancellation penalties and exact names of the airlines and hotels included in the package.
- If a charter flight is involved, ask for the charter operator's

name and address and then check its registration with the U.S. Department of Transportation and Office of Consumer Affairs in Washington, D.C.

- Be suspicious of vacation certificates that claim you have "won" a hotel stay or resort visit. If you have to pay something to get the promised "free" vacation, stay away.
- Never give credit card information over the phone to a company or person you're not familiar with.
- Use reputable travel agents or Internet travel sites.

Have a good time, but you may want to throw this book in the glove box for quick reference, just in case you have other immediate needs such as bonding out of jail. Otherwise, have fun and try to be as safe as you can.

Travel abroad — actually prepare: Well, let's say it's spring break and your buddies have convinced you to leave the United States, or they're talking about backpacking through Europe this summer. What should you do if you think you may join them? Start getting ready now. Passports and travel visas don't just fall from the sky. Governmental bureaucracy and the red tape that comes with it takes time. With the "war on terrorism," travel has become even more tricky.

This section has been drawn from reviewing many resources, but most has been taken directly from the Department of State's Bureau of Consular Affairs, aimed at students who are planning to travel or study abroad.

If you do nothing else, become familiar with the basic laws and customs of the country you plan to visit and do a little research about the people, their culture and any problems that the country is experiencing that could affect your travel plans. A little local knowledge may keep you on the road and out of a foreign jail. The Department of State publishes Background Notes on about 170 countries. These brief, factual pamphlets contain information on each country's culture, history, geography, economy, government, and current political situation. Background Notes are available at state.gov. Bookstores and the school library, not to mention the Internet, should provide ample information about any part of the world you want to see.

Find out what information your school offers for students who are planning to study, travel, or work abroad. Student advisers can provide you with information about studying or working abroad and may also be able to provide you with information on how to save money on transportation, lodging, hostels and other things you might need to know.

If you are booking through a travel company, find out what it offers before plunking down a deposit. Most private programs for vacation, study or work abroad are reputable and financially sound, but some have been known to charge exorbitant fees, use deliberately false "educational" claims and describe working conditions that turn out to be far from the truth. Don't get taken.

Consular Information Sheets also provide updated travel information on any country in the world, including its entry regulations, crime and security assessments, drug laws and penalties, road conditions and where you can find the U.S. embassy, consulates, and consular agencies. Also check for Travel Warnings and Public Announcements, which make recommendations that may suggest U.S. citizens defer travel to a country because of dangerous conditions.

Check these out at travel.state.gov or by calling the Office of Overseas Citizens Services at 202-647-5225. By mail, send a self-addressed, stamped business-size envelope to:

Overseas Citizens Services
Room 4811, Department of State
Washington, D.C., 20520-4818

Passports and visas: Passports are required to enter and/or depart most countries. Apply for a passport as soon as possible. Some countries also require U.S. citizens to obtain a visa before entering. A passport is an internationally recognized travel document attesting to your identity and nationality. In essence, it is a request by our government that officials of foreign governments permit you to travel or sojourn in their territories and to afford you lawful aid and protection.

A passport is not required for travel by U.S. citizens to territories subject to the jurisdiction of the United States (including Puerto Rico, Guam, American Samoa and the U.S. Virgin Islands), but everywhere else requires a passport (including Mexico and Canada).

A passport and a visa are not the same and most countries require visitors who are planning to study or work abroad to obtain visas before entering. A visa is an endorsement or stamp placed by officials of a foreign country on a U.S. passport that allows the bearer to visit that foreign country. Basically, a visa is permission granted by the government of a country to a non-citizen to enter that country and to remain for a specific period of time. It is the responsibility of the traveler to obtain necessary visas, if any, before proceeding abroad. Visas can be obtained from the embassy or consulate of the countries to which the applicant wishes to travel, but don't wait until the last second. It can take weeks to get a visa.

I need a passport. How do I get one? To obtain a passport, you need to go to an acceptance agent with two passport photographs of yourself, a certified copy of your birth certificate and a valid form of photo identification, such as a driver's license. You will find the passport application there. The normal processing fee is $60 for adults 16 or older and $40 for applicants younger than 16. Payment may be made in cash, by credit or debit card or by personal check for the full amount. You will have to personally visit a post office or courthouse to apply for a passport unless you are filing for a renewal. (See questions below on renewals.) During peak travel periods, the normal processing time ranges from four to six weeks, but if you need a passport more quickly, you may use an expedited service, which takes two to three weeks.

Do I need to renew my passport? If you have already had a passport issued and you answer yes to all of these questions you can renew your passport:

- I can submit my most recent passport.
- I was at least 16 when my most recent passport was issued.
- I was issued my most recent passport less than 15 years ago.

- I use the same name as on my most recent passport, OR, I have had my name changed by marriage or court order and can submit proper documentation to reflect my name changes.

If you do not have a copy of your birth certificate, you will have to contact the proper agency in the state of your birth and order a vital record. If there is no official record of your birth, you will need to contact the proper agency of your birth state. A letter will be issued to this fact. Then other items can be used for proof. If you are a naturalized citizen, the original naturalization certificate must accompany the application for a passport and will be returned by the passport agency. If you are not a U.S. citizen and need a passport, you will need to contact the nearest consulate for your country.

If your passport has been lost, stolen or mutilated, you must complete a new application, the DS-11, with new pictures, birth certificate and affidavit of lost or stolen passport. The affidavit is form DS-64, available through acceptance agents.

If you are a convicted felon, it is entirely up to the discretion of the passport agency whether you can get one or not.

"That's not mine!" To cap off your spring break in Acapulco, Joe suggests that the "excellent" "kind bud" Acapulco Gold he scored on the beach should not go to waste and that one of you should hide it in your bag for the flight home.

What could it hurt? It's just a little bit and it would be great back at school. It should now begin to become clear that this is not a good idea and may result in the "holder" to a strip search, body cavity search and federal or state drug charges. Even a small amount can cause big problems. It's not worth it!

This general rule applies to all foreign and domestic travel. Laws in other countries can be much more harsh than what you may think, so don't fool around with the thought. The results can be quite similar, however foreign jails are usually much less comfortable than those here in the states. Watch the movie *Midnight Express* for further details.

Another excellent rule to live by is to never carry anything through customs for someone else without knowing exactly what it is. Your trusting nature could result in an unpleasant circumstance. Again, not worth it!

"I'm in another country; I'm in trouble; who do I call?" If you are in trouble or arrested, run into civil unrest, or simply need some advice, find the location of the nearest U.S. embassy or consulate and even register with the consular section when you arrive, if possible. (U.S. embassy and consulate locations can be found in the country's consular information sheet.) If your family needs to reach you because of an emergency, they can pass a message to you through the Office of Overseas Citizens Services at 202-647-5225, which will contact the embassy or consulate in the country where you are traveling and pass a message from your family to you. Remember consular officers cannot cash checks, lend money or serve as your attorney, but they can, if the need arises, assist you in obtaining emergency funds from your family, help you find an attorney or medical assistance, and replace your lost or stolen passport.

CONCLUSION

LIKE WE TALKED ABOUT at the beginning of this book, knowledge is power. The more you know, the better prepared you are to deal with whatever situation you may find yourself. I hope that this book answered some of the questions you may have had, as well as some you may not have even thought about. Although this book is not intended to be legal advice, it should at least give you some insight into what the law is in certain situations and help you conduct yourself within the law. One important thing to remember is don't ever use the law as a tool to take advantage of someone. The laws of our state are there to be fair and make sure everyone knows what they should or should not do.

If you are unsure about your rights, the law, or how to get something done, contact an attorney and seek professional help. Most reputable lawyers will at least sit down and talk with you, at no charge, to at least see what, if any, legal help you need. Your school may also have an attorney on staff for that exact purpose, so find out and make sure you protect yourself under the law.

With this knowledge, you will hopefully not suffer the pitfalls some college students fall into, usually without ever knowing what they are. So work, study and play hard.

Enjoy your time in college. If you take advantage of this great time, you should move on to enjoy a successful life, whatever you choose to do with it.

INDEX

ABOUT THE AUTHOR

Scot Courtney received a Bachelor of Arts degree from what is now Texas State University in 1990 and his Juris Doctorate from Thurgood Marshall School of Law in 1994, where he was a member of the Law Review. Board Certified by the Texas Board of Legal Specialization in Criminal Law, he has defended clients in more than 200 courts around the state. Courtney is an active member of the Association of Trial Lawyers of America, Texas Criminal Defense Lawyers Association, Harris County Criminal Defense Lawyers Association, Travis County Criminal Defense Lawyer's Association and Hays County Bar Association. He lives in San Marcos with his wife and son.